Unshakeable Faith- 31 Days of Peace in God's Word

Joshua Rhoades

Published by Joshua Paul Rhoades, 2024.

While every precaution has been taken in the preparation of this book, the publisher assumes no responsibility for errors or omissions, or for damages resulting from the use of the information contained herein.

UNSHAKEABLE FAITH- 31 DAYS OF PEACE IN GOD'S WORD

First edition. October 25, 2024.

Copyright © 2024 Joshua Rhoades.

ISBN: 979-8224227419

Written by Joshua Rhoades.

Also by Joshua Rhoades

Courage Under Fire: David's Stand On The Battlefield

Jonah's Journey: Voices Of Redemption And Lessons In Obedience

The Furnace Of Faith: 12 Principles From The Heat Of Faith

Whispers of Hope: Inspiring Stories of Men's Prayers In Scripture

Frontier Legends: The Oregon Dream

Elijah: A Beacon Of Boldness

HOOK, LINE & SAVIOUR - Faith Reflections from Fishing

Driven By Faith: Motor Racing Inspired Christian Life

30 Day Devotional - Bold and Strong- Coffee Devotions for a Courageous Christian Walk

Authentic Christianity: The Heart of Old Time Religion

Consider The Ant - God's Tiny Preachers

Flee Fornication: The Plea For Purity

Renewed Hope- How to Find Encouragement in God

Sounding The Call - The Voice of Conviction

The Altar - Where Heaven Meets Earth

The Bible's Battlefields- Timeless Lessons from Ancient Wars

The Sacred Art of Silence - How Silence Speaks in Scripture

Under Fire- The Sanctity of the Traditional Biblical Home

Who Is on the Lord's Side? A Call to Righteousness

What Is Truth? - From Skepticism to Submission

First and Goal- Faith and Football Fundamentals

From Dugout to Devotion- Spiritual Lessons from Baseball

Par for the Course- Faith and Fairways

The Believer's Pace- Tools for Running Life's Marathon

The Immutable Fortress- Security in God's Unchanging Nature

Biblical Bravery

Deer Stands and Devotions: A Hunter's Walk with God

Jesus Knows- Our Hearts, Our Responsibility
Restoration - Setting The Bone
Spiritual 911- God's Word for Life's Emergency's
The Freedom of Forgiveness
The Jezebel Effect - Ancient Manipulations Modern Lessons
The Shout That Stopped The Saviour
The Time Machine Chronicles: Old Testament Characters
Anchored In Truth Exploring The Depths of Psalm 119
Biblical Counsel on Anger
Proverbs' Portraits The Men God Mentions
Stumbling in the Dark - The Dangers of Alcohol
Guarding the Wicket Protecting Your Faith and Game
The Champion's Faith - Wrestling and Achieving Spiritual Victory
Scriptural Commands for Modern Times Living God's Word Today Volume 1
Scriptural Commands for Modern Times Living God's Word Today Volume 2
Scriptural Commands for Modern Times Living God's Word TodayVolume3
The Greatest Gift
A Christmas Journey of Faith
Daughter Of The King: Embracing Your Identity In Christ
Determination and Dedication Building Strong Faith As A Young Man
Walking Through Walls God's Power to Part the Storms of Life
David's Song Of Deliverance Praising God Through Every Storm
From Weakness to Warrior: Gideon's Transformation
Why Did Jesus Weep?
Living For God The Call To Be A Living Sacrifice
My Mind Is In A Fog What Do I Do?
Turning The Page Written By Grace
The Calling and Greatness of John the Baptist
For Such a Time Esther's Courageous Stand
From Brokenness To Beauty Written By The Pen of Grace
The Ultimate Guide to Massive Action- From Plans to Reality
A Heart Of Conviction
Serving In The Shadows
Repentance Revealed The Road Back To God
The Chief Sinner Meets The Chief Saviour Reflections On I Timothy 1:15

Answer The Call - 31 Days of Biblical Action

The Birthmark of the Believer

Reflections on Calvary's Cross

The Kingdom Builder Paul's Bold Proclamation of Christ

The Animal Of Pride

The Reach That Restores Christ Love For The Broken

Paul- The Many Roles of a Servant of Christ

Unshakeable Faith- 31 Days of Peace in God's Word

Dedication

To you, dear reader, this book is dedicated with heartfelt hope and encouragement, that as you journey through these 31 days, you will find a peace that roots deep into your soul, a peace that stands strong no matter the storm. In a world full of noise, worry, and uncertainty, you have taken a beautiful step toward finding the quiet strength and steadfast assurance that only God can provide. This devotional is more than a book; it's a friend on the path, a place to rest and be reminded of truths that never change. May each page bring you closer to the unwavering love of God, who knows your heart fully and is eager to fill it with His peace. No matter what you face, His Word promises to hold you steady. Remember, you are not alone. Every line here is written with you in mind, for every person who has longed for calm in the chaos, for assurance in the unknown. As you read, may you feel God's presence drawing near, wrapping you in comfort, giving you courage, and filling you with hope that cannot be shaken. Know that every moment spent with Him is a moment of peace, and that His promises are a solid foundation on which to stand. Each day as you open this book, let your heart open too, allowing His words to touch the places that need healing, strength, and encouragement. God's love is unending, His faithfulness is forever, and His peace is always available, right here for you. May you find that by the end of this journey, your faith feels stronger, your heart feels lighter, and you know with certainty that you are deeply loved and securely held by God. This dedication is my prayer for you—that you'll discover a faith that is unshakeable and a peace that no circumstance can take away.

Introduction

In a world that often feels uncertain and overwhelming, "Unshakeable Faith: 31 Days of Peace in God's Word" is here to remind us of the steady, unchanging hope we have in God. Every day, we face challenges—some small, some that shake us to our core—but no matter what we're up against, God's Word promises that we can have peace and security in Him. This book isn't just another devotional; it's a journey through 31 days of finding comfort, encouragement, and the assurance that we are never alone. Through each day's reading, you'll discover reasons why God's presence gives us a peace that cannot be moved, no matter the storms we face. Right now, the world seems more uncertain than ever. There's worry in the news, fears about the future, and personal struggles that weigh heavily on our hearts. It's easy to feel overwhelmed or to lose sight of the hope we have in Christ. But this is exactly why we need to hold onto God's promises with unshakeable faith. This devotional was created to help us remember that God is our rock, our refuge, and our strength, and that He promises to carry us through every challenge we encounter. Each day, "Unshakeable Faith" draws us back to God's Word, showing us that His peace is not just a feeling but a truth that we can stand on. This peace comes from knowing that God is in control and that His love for us never changes. His promises are sure, His presence is real, and His power is greater than any fear we face. As we open our hearts to His Word, we begin to see that this peace is not based on our circumstances but on our relationship with a God who is always faithful. This book is a reminder that our faith, when rooted in God, is stronger than anything life can throw at us. Every day, "Unshakeable Faith" invites us to let go of our anxieties and rest in God's love, to replace our fears with trust, and to remember that God's peace is always available to us. It encourages us to build a faith that doesn't waver when life is hard but instead grows stronger. It's time to allow God's Word to guide us, reassure us, and give us the courage to face each day with hope, knowing that our souls can truly say, "It is well." In these times, we need an unshakeable faith more than ever, a faith that reminds us that no matter what we face, we can have peace in God's promises, today and always.

Chapter 1 - Divine Love

Romans 8:38-39 tells us of a love so powerful, so deep, and so unwavering that nothing in all creation can separate us from it: "For I am persuaded, that neither death, nor life...shall be able to separate us from the love of God, which is in Christ Jesus our Lord." This Scripture speaks of the Divine Love of God, a love so complete and strong that no force, no hardship, no height nor depth, nor any creature or trial, can ever pull us away from it. This love is not like human love, which can sometimes fail or falter; this is the love of God Himself, everlasting and steadfast, reaching out to us in every moment, whether we are walking in joy or trudging through sorrow. God's love for us is not just a concept; it is a living, breathing reality. He loves us so completely that He sent His only Son, Jesus, to live, suffer, and die for us, showing us that His love is beyond words. Even though we may feel unworthy, even though we sometimes fail or fall, this love is constant and unfailing, embracing us in our brokenness and lifting us up in His grace. It is this love that reassures us in our darkest times, reminding us that we are never alone, that God is always with us, and that nothing can take His love away from us. Not life with all its pressures, nor death with all its fear, not the angels above nor any power below, nothing in the entire universe has the strength to sever this bond of love God has with His children. God's love in Christ is our anchor, holding us steady in every storm, surrounding us in every struggle, comforting us in every loss, and giving us hope beyond every disappointment. This love is not conditional, waiting for us to be perfect or sinless; it is unconditional, a free gift given to us because God is love itself. Jesus' sacrifice on the cross was the ultimate demonstration of this love—a love that overcomes sin, heals wounds, breaks chains, and restores hearts. Even when we doubt ourselves, even when we feel lost or unlovable, this love holds onto us and reminds us of our worth in God's eyes. It is a love that forgives, that believes in us, and that gives us the strength to face each day with

courage and joy. This Divine Love promises that no matter what we face, we have a Savior who walks with us, a God who calls us His own, and a Father who treasures us beyond measure. The depth, height, width, and length of God's love are boundless, more than we can ever fully understand, but we can rest in knowing that it is real, eternal, and ours to receive. This love is the reason we can live in hope, the reason we can find peace in uncertainty, and the reason we can stand firm in faith, knowing that our Creator and Redeemer holds us close. Nothing we go through can take us out of His hand, and nothing we face can separate us from His embrace. This Divine Love in Christ is our assurance, our foundation, and our future, an unbreakable bond that spans beyond time and fills us with the confidence that we are fully loved, now and forever.

Chapter 2 - Deliverance from Sin

In Colossians 1:14, we are given a beautiful and powerful promise: "In whom we have redemption through his blood, even the forgiveness of sins." This verse speaks to the incredible gift of Deliverance from Sin that Jesus Christ has given to every one of us through His sacrifice. From the very beginning of time, sin has been a burden that no human could bear or remove alone; it separated us from God, weighed us down with guilt, and brought pain and suffering into the world. But in His perfect love, God made a way for us to be free from sin forever. Through the blood of Jesus, we are offered redemption—a complete and total release from the power of sin over our lives. Jesus, the Son of God, willingly took our place on the cross, bearing the weight of every sin, every wrong, every failure we would ever commit, and through His death and resurrection, He made forgiveness possible. His blood cleanses us, washes us whiter than snow, and breaks every chain that sin once had over us. We are no longer prisoners to our mistakes, our past, or our shame because Jesus paid the price in full. This deliverance is not something we have to earn or work for; it is a gift freely given by a loving Savior who wants us to live in freedom and peace. Redemption means that we have been bought back, that we are no longer owned by sin or darkness, but we belong to God. His forgiveness is complete—it does not just cover some sins and leave others; it forgives them all, fully and completely. When God forgives us, He casts our sins as far as the east is from the west, and He remembers them no more. This truth is a source of hope and joy for us, knowing that we don't have to live in the shadows of our past mistakes or failures. Jesus' blood has broken the curse of sin, and we are free to walk in the light of His love, knowing that we are forgiven, loved, and accepted. The forgiveness of sins means that we are no longer separated from God; we are reconciled to Him, brought back into a close and loving relationship with our Creator. This deliverance from sin is a new beginning for each of us, a fresh start, where we are no longer defined by what we have done wrong but by who we are in Christ. Because of His redemption, we can approach God with confidence, knowing that we are covered by the righteousness of Jesus, and we are no longer condemned. Deliverance from sin means that we are empowered to live differently, to turn away from what once held us captive, and to walk in the newness of life that Jesus has given us. This redemption through His blood is the foundation of our faith, the reason we can have peace and joy in every circumstance, because we know that our sins are forgiven and that we are set free. It is a gift that fills our hearts with gratitude and humbles us, as we remember that Jesus endured the cross for our sakes. This deliverance from sin is available to everyone; no one is beyond God's reach, and no sin is too great for His forgiveness. When we accept this gift of redemption, we are transformed, made new, and given a future full of hope and promise. The deliverance that Jesus provides is everlasting; it is not something that fades or can be taken away—it is secure in Him. Because of His blood, we are children of God, saved by grace, and set free to live in the fullness of His love. This deliverance from sin is a reminder of God's incredible mercy and His desire for each of us to live in the freedom that only He can provide.

Chapter 3 - Daily Mercies

In Lamentations 3:22, we find one of the most comforting promises in Scripture: "It is of the LORD's mercies that we are not consumed, because his compassions fail not." This verse reveals the beauty of Daily Mercies—the unending grace and love God showers upon us every single day. Life can be hard, and we all face moments where we feel weak, burdened, or even broken. We make mistakes, we stumble, and at times we might feel unworthy or far from God. Yet, every morning, God's mercies are new, and His compassion never fails us. Each day, despite our flaws, He chooses to show us kindness, forgiveness, and strength to keep going. These daily mercies mean that no matter what happened yesterday, God is ready to give us a fresh start today. His mercy is like a soft blanket of grace that covers us, holding us up when we feel like we're falling, healing us when we feel broken, and restoring our souls when we feel weary. His compassion is so deep and endless that He sees our struggles, understands our pain, and never grows tired of being there for us. Imagine the kindness of a Father who knows every mistake we make and every weakness we hold but still offers us love and patience without end. We are not consumed by life's trials, nor are we destroyed by our sins, because God's mercy is stronger than all of it. This mercy is not something we can earn; it is a gift that God offers us out of His boundless love. Every day, He looks at us with compassion and says, "You are loved, forgiven, and worthy." The Lord's mercies are like a river that never runs dry, flowing into our lives with grace, filling us with hope and courage to face whatever comes. Even when we feel undeserving, His mercy reaches us, reminding us that we are precious in His eyes. Because of these daily mercies, we have the strength to get up each morning, knowing that no matter what happens, God's love will carry us through. His compassions are unfailing; they never lessen or run out. Every time we need Him, He is there, ready to lift us up, to forgive us, and to guide us back to His heart. His mercy renews us, giving us a chance to leave behind our past mistakes and walk forward in hope. When we truly understand this mercy, it changes everything. We no longer have to live in fear or shame, because God's mercy covers us. We no longer have to doubt His love, because His compassion is steadfast, eternal, and stronger than any mistake we could make. Every morning, we are greeted with a love that says, "Today is a new day; today, you are forgiven." And because of these daily mercies, we are able to extend mercy to others, showing them the same kindness and compassion that God shows to us. These mercies remind us that God is not just a distant ruler but a loving Father who walks with us, who cares deeply for us, and who offers us the grace we need to keep going, no matter what.

Chapter 4 - Divine Protection

In Psalm 34:7, we are given a beautiful promise of Divine Protection, as it says, "The angel of the LORD encampeth round about them that fear him, and delivereth them." This verse reminds us of the comforting truth that God, in His infinite power and love, surrounds His children with protection that cannot be broken. It is not just any protection; it is His divine and heavenly protection, the kind that goes beyond human understanding. Imagine being encircled by the angel of the Lord, knowing that God Himself has set up a shield around you, guarding you from harm. This isn't just a promise for ancient times; it is a living, active promise for all who place their trust in Him. His protection is always with us, even when we cannot see it. We may face danger, uncertainty, or fear, but we are never alone, for God's angels surround us. They are like an army, encamping around us wherever we go. Each day, whether we are at home, at school, at work, or traveling, God's angels are with us, keeping us safe. We may not always be aware of their presence, but they are there, fighting battles we cannot see, standing between us and harm. God's protection is powerful; it shields us from both visible and invisible threats. The enemy may try to attack, but he cannot penetrate the barrier that God has placed around His children. This protection is not because of anything we have done to earn it, but because of God's love and faithfulness. His angels are on guard, ready to deliver us in times of trouble, lifting us out of situations that would otherwise bring us harm. This promise means we can walk in peace, even in the midst of chaos, knowing that God's protection surrounds us like a fortress. We may face trials, but God's angels are watching over us, and they will not allow us to be overwhelmed. Just as a shepherd watches over his flock, so does God watch over us, making sure we are safe and secure. His divine protection is not just for moments of great danger but is with us every moment of every day. When we trust in Him, we can rest in the assurance that no harm will come to us without passing through His loving hands. He holds us in His arms, and His angels encircle us, creating a refuge we can run to in any storm. Even when life seems uncertain, we can stand firm, knowing that we are protected by the Creator of the universe. This Divine Protection is a reminder that we are never alone, and that God is always watching over us, providing a shield that no enemy can penetrate. It is His love that encamps around us, His mercy that delivers us, and His strength that keeps us safe.

Chapter 5 - Dependence on His Strength

In Philippians 4:13, we read the powerful words, "I can do all things through Christ which strengtheneth me," a promise that fills us with courage and reminds us of our absolute Dependence on His Strength. This verse speaks to every heart, reminding us that we are not alone in our struggles or challenges. In our human strength, we often feel weak, overwhelmed, and even incapable of facing what life throws at us. Yet, this verse tells us that with Christ, we are more than enough because His strength fills every gap in our weakness, lifts us when we fall, and empowers us to keep going when we want to give up. Life is full of moments that test us, whether it's a difficult situation at school, a tough time at work, a challenge in our family, or a struggle in our personal lives. Sometimes, we may feel like we are carrying burdens too heavy to bear, but in these moments, Christ's strength becomes our lifeline. It is His power that gives us the ability to persevere, to rise above every trial, and to find victory, even in situations that seem impossible. This strength from Christ is not just a boost of energy; it is a steady, unbreakable power that supports us through every season of life. It is not temporary; it is enduring and everlasting. It allows us to face every mountain, cross every valley, and overcome every obstacle with confidence, because we know that we are not relying on our own limited abilities but on the infinite strength of our Savior. Jesus doesn't just help us from a distance; He is within us, filling us with His strength, empowering us from the inside out. He knows every weakness we have, every area where we feel incapable, and He promises to be our source of strength, our anchor, and our guide. With Christ, we can do things we never thought possible, whether it's forgiving someone who has hurt us, stepping out in faith to follow our dreams, or standing firm in our faith when the world around us is unsteady. His strength doesn't mean we won't face difficulties, but it does mean that we can walk through them with confidence, knowing that Christ is with us every step of the way. He is the rock that keeps us steady, the friend who never leaves, and the Savior who empowers us to do all things according to His will. We may be weak, but He is strong, and because of His strength, we can face each day with courage and hope. We are never asked to face life alone, for Christ is always with us, providing the strength we need exactly when we need it. When we feel like giving up, His strength lifts us; when we feel lost, His strength guides us; and when we feel defeated, His strength renews us. With Christ, there is nothing we cannot overcome, nothing too hard to endure, and nothing impossible to achieve. Our dependence on His strength is not a sign of weakness; it is the key to living a life full of purpose, resilience, and faith. His strength is our comfort, our peace, and our power, and in Him, we find everything we need to live boldly, joyfully, and victoriously. Christ's strength is a gift that fills us with hope and courage, reminding us every day that, with Him, all things are truly possible.

Chapter 6 - Depth of His Peace

In John 14:27, Jesus offers us a promise that is both beautiful and powerful: "Peace I leave with you, my peace I give unto you... Let not your heart be troubled." These words reveal the Depth of His Peace, a peace that goes beyond what we can understand, a peace that fills us with comfort and calm even when everything around us feels chaotic. The peace Jesus gives is not like the temporary relief that the world offers; it is a lasting, unshakable peace that holds us steady through every storm, every heartache, every moment of fear or doubt. Jesus' peace is His gift to us, given freely and abundantly to calm our troubled hearts and settle our restless minds. When He says, "Let not your heart be troubled," He is inviting us to lay down our worries, to let go of our anxieties, and to rest in His presence. The depth of His peace reaches into the very core of our souls, offering a quiet assurance that no matter what happens, we are safe in His hands. This peace doesn't mean that we will never face difficulties, but it does mean that we don't have to face them alone or with fear. His peace is like a strong anchor that holds us in place, a gentle voice that calms our fears, and a soft embrace that wraps around us, reminding us that He is with us always. Even when we walk through dark valleys, even when life feels overwhelming, His peace is there, giving us the strength to breathe, to trust, and to move forward with courage. Jesus understands every burden we carry, every fear we face, and every worry that troubles our hearts, and in His love, He offers us peace that can carry us through it all. The depth of His peace reminds us that we don't have to have all the answers, because we know the One who does. His peace gives us the confidence to face each day, the calm to quiet our racing thoughts, and the assurance that He is in control, no matter how uncertain things may seem. With Jesus' peace, we can stand strong, knowing that He has overcome the world and that nothing can separate us from His love. This peace fills the empty places, heals the broken parts, and lifts the heavy burdens, reminding us that we are deeply loved and held by the Prince of Peace. Jesus' peace doesn't change our circumstances, but it changes us, giving us a quiet joy that sustains us, a calm that keeps us steady, and a hope that lights our way. When we accept this peace, our hearts find rest, and our souls find refuge, because we know that Jesus is with us, and His peace is more than enough. Let not your heart be troubled, for His peace is always with you, as deep, powerful, and everlasting as His love.

Chapter 7 - Dedication to His Word

Psalm 119:105 tells us, "Thy word is a lamp unto my feet, and a light unto my path," and these words reveal the beauty and power of Dedication to His Word. God's Word is not just a book of stories or commands; it is a living guide, a source of strength, and a wellspring of wisdom that lights up our way in this often-dark world. His Word is the light that shows us where to step, especially when we feel unsure or confused. It is like a lamp that shines right in front of us, giving us just enough light for each step we take. When we commit ourselves to His Word, we find direction for every situation, strength for every struggle, and answers for every question. In a world that can feel overwhelming or full of distractions, God's Word is our anchor, helping us to stand firm and stay true to what is right. By dedicating ourselves to reading, studying, and loving His Word, we draw closer to God Himself. His words reveal His heart, His will, and His promises, and when we hold onto them, they bring comfort, hope, and peace. His Word teaches us how to live, how to love, and how to serve others with compassion and grace. It warns us of dangers, reminds us of His love, and assures us of His presence. It's like a friend who is always with us, guiding us in truth and never leading us astray. Every time we open the Bible, we step into the presence of God, hearing His voice and feeling His love through the pages. Even when the world is confusing, His Word remains clear, steady, and true. The Bible tells us what is right and wrong, helps us see ourselves as God sees us, and reminds us that we are deeply loved. With His Word as our guide, we can face any challenge, for we know that we are walking in God's ways. It strengthens us when we are weak, gives us courage when we are afraid, and fills us with hope when we are down. His Word is not just a rule book; it is a letter from a loving Father to His children, a message of love, hope, and purpose. When we dedicate ourselves to His Word, we find that we are never alone, for God Himself is with us, speaking to us, teaching us, and leading

us along the path He has set. His Word is alive, and it breathes life into our hearts, filling us with faith and joy. It helps us make wise decisions, keeps us on the right path, and leads us closer to God every day. With every verse, we see more of who God is and who we are meant to be. We discover that His Word is our protection, our encouragement, and our truth. No matter how dark the world may seem, His Word is the light that never goes out, the lamp that never dims, and the guide that never leads us wrong. Dedicating ourselves to His Word means we are choosing to live in His light, to walk in His truth, and to follow His voice, no matter where it may lead. In every season, in every trial, and in every joy, His Word is our constant companion, our faithful guide, and our unchanging hope.

Chapter 8 - Direction for Life

In Proverbs 3:5-6, we are given one of the most reassuring promises for life: "Trust in the LORD with all thine heart; and lean not unto thine own understanding. In all thy ways acknowledge him, and he shall direct thy paths." These words remind us of the incredible peace, wisdom, and security that comes from placing our lives fully in God's hands. Direction for Life is not something we have to figure out on our own, nor is it left to chance. God promises that if we trust Him fully, He will guide us through every season, every situation, and every challenge. To trust in the Lord with all our heart means giving Him our deepest hopes, our biggest fears, our unknowns, and even our doubts. Trusting Him completely means surrendering every part of ourselves, not just the parts that are easy or that feel comfortable. It means having faith that God's way is always better than our own, even when we can't see the full picture or understand why He's leading us a certain way. Life is full of choices, twists, and challenges, and there are times when we may feel uncertain or lost, unsure of the path we should take. But this verse offers us a promise: if we lean on God rather than our own understanding, He will direct our paths.

This direction from God isn't just for the big moments—like choosing a career, finding a spouse, or facing a major decision; it's also for the daily steps, the small decisions, and the little moments that make up our lives. God cares about every single aspect of our journey, and He is always there, ready to guide us. His promise to direct our paths is a reminder that we don't have to walk alone. When we acknowledge Him in all our ways, we're inviting Him to be a part of everything we do. Acknowledging God means making Him a part of our thoughts, our actions, and our choices. It's about saying, "God, I trust that Your way is best, and I'm willing to follow where You lead." It's a powerful act of surrender, one that allows God's wisdom to take the place of our limited understanding.

God's direction is perfect, because He knows our needs, our purpose, and the unique path that He has planned for each of us. Unlike our own understanding, which can be flawed or short-sighted, God's wisdom is limitless. He sees the entire picture of our lives, from beginning to end, and He knows the best path for us to take. He can see obstacles we cannot see, and He understands our strengths and weaknesses better than we do. Trusting in Him to direct our paths means that we are choosing to follow the One who knows us better than we know ourselves. It's choosing to trust that God's love for us is so deep and so real that He will never lead us astray. His direction is always rooted in His love, His wisdom, and His perfect will for our lives.

Sometimes, trusting God with our direction means letting go of our own plans or dreams. There may be times when we think we know what's best for us, but God has something different, and ultimately better, in mind. Trusting Him means being willing to lay down our own desires when they don't align with His will, believing that His plans for us are far greater than anything we could imagine for ourselves. This is not always easy, especially when we're facing uncertainty or when we don't understand why things are happening the way they are. But Proverbs 3:5-6 calls us to trust God with all our heart, not just part of it. It's a call to have complete confidence in His wisdom and goodness, even when our circumstances feel confusing or painful.

As we trust in God's direction, we find a peace that surpasses all understanding. This peace doesn't come from knowing every answer or having everything figured out; it comes from knowing that God is in control. When we put our trust in Him, we can walk in peace, even in the midst of life's challenges, because we know that our steps are guided by a loving and faithful God. This peace is a gift that comes from surrendering our worries, our fears, and our anxieties to Him. It is a peace that assures us that, no matter what happens, we are safe in His hands. We don't have to carry the weight of figuring out our future or controlling every outcome, because we have a Father who promises to lead us every step of the way.

God's direction for our lives is something that we can rely on in every season. In times of joy and success, we can acknowledge Him by giving thanks and using our blessings to serve others. In times of struggle and uncertainty, we can lean on Him, knowing that He will guide us through. His direction doesn't mean that we will never face hard times, but it does mean that we never have to face them alone. He walks with us through every valley, every trial, and every moment of doubt, providing strength, comfort, and guidance. When we trust in God's direction, we are choosing to let Him be our Shepherd, leading us to green pastures and still waters, restoring our souls, and guiding us on the path of righteousness.

This trust is a daily choice, one that we must make over and over again. There will be times when we are tempted to rely on our own understanding, to take control, or to go our own way. But each time we choose to trust in the Lord, we are building a foundation of faith that grows stronger and deeper. We are learning to walk by faith and not by sight, to rely on God's wisdom rather than our own, and to find joy in His guidance. Trusting in God's direction means believing that He is working all things together for our good, even when we can't see it in the moment. It's trusting that His ways are higher than our ways, and that His thoughts are higher than our thoughts.

When we truly trust in God, we can let go of the fear of making the wrong choices or taking the wrong path. We don't have to worry about missing out on God's plan, because He is faithful to guide us. His promise is not that He will give us every detail of our future but that He will be with us, leading us step by step. Sometimes, His direction comes in the form of a gentle nudge or a quiet whisper, while other times, it may come through the wise counsel of others or through doors He opens or closes. No matter how He chooses to lead us, we can be confident that He will keep His promise to direct our paths.

Trusting in God's direction also means that we are not defined by our past mistakes. Even if we have taken wrong turns or made choices we regret, God is able to redirect our steps and bring us back to the path He has for us. His grace covers our failures, and His mercy is new every morning. When we turn to Him and ask for guidance, He is always there, ready to lead us forward. No mistake is too big for God to forgive, and no detour is too far for Him to redeem. He is the God of second chances, and His direction for our lives is always one of hope, healing, and restoration.

God's promise to direct our paths is a reminder that He is deeply invested in our lives. He doesn't just set us on a path and leave us to figure it out on our own; He walks with us, guiding us, correcting us, and encouraging us along the way. His direction is not a burden but a blessing, a gift that brings us closer to Him and helps us grow in faith. As we trust in Him, we find that His way is not only right but also fulfilling and full of joy. His direction leads us to a life that is rich in purpose, peace, and love, a life that reflects His goodness and brings glory to His name.

In every season, whether we are facing joy or sorrow, success or failure, clarity or confusion, God's direction is constant. He is the Good Shepherd, the loving Father, and the wise King who knows our hearts, our desires, and our needs. When we trust Him with all our heart, we are inviting Him to lead us into the life He has prepared for us, a life that is greater than anything we could imagine for ourselves. His plans for us are good, and His purpose for us is filled with hope and a future.

As we continue to place our trust in the Lord, He continues to direct our paths, guiding us with His wisdom, covering us with His grace, and filling us with His peace. Each day, we have the choice to trust Him more, to surrender our understanding, and to follow His lead with confidence and joy. And as we do, we will find that God's direction is perfect, His love is unfailing, and His guidance is a constant source of strength and hope. We don't have to fear the future, because we know that God is already there, preparing the way for us and leading us with His unfailing love.

Chapter 9 - Deliverance from Fear

In 2 Timothy 1:7, we are given one of the most empowering promises for every heart that battles fear: "For God hath not given us the spirit of fear; but of power, and of love, and of a sound mind." These words remind us that Deliverance from Fear is not only possible but is a gift that God Himself gives to us. Fear is something that tries to creep into every part of our lives—it tries to limit us, to make us doubt, to steal our joy, and to hold us back from all that God has planned for us. Yet, here, we are told that God has not given us this spirit of fear; it doesn't come from Him, and it has no place in a heart that trusts in the Lord. Instead, God fills us with three incredible gifts: power, love, and a sound mind. The power that God gives us is His own strength within us, giving us the courage to face every situation, every challenge, and every uncertainty without fear. It's the strength to rise above our worries, to stand firm in our faith, and to know that we are never alone, for God Himself is with us. When we feel weak, when we feel scared, or when we feel overwhelmed, God's power becomes our foundation, reminding us that we can do all things through Him. This power is not from ourselves; it is a divine strength that fills us and gives us the confidence to face each day, knowing that we are held and supported by the Almighty. Along with this power, God gives us the gift of love—a love that is greater than any fear. Perfect love, the Bible tells us, casts out fear, and God's love is truly perfect. It surrounds us, fills us, and reminds us that we are precious, valued, and deeply loved by our Creator. His love for us is so strong that it protects us, gives us peace, and assures us that nothing in all creation can separate us from Him. This love pushes out the fear in our hearts, replacing it with security and peace, because we know that we are safe in the arms of God. Finally, God gives us a sound mind—a mind that is calm, clear, and focused on His truth. Fear tries to cloud our thoughts, to make us anxious, to fill us with doubts, but a sound mind from God brings clarity and peace. It helps us focus

on His promises rather than on our worries, to see His hand in every situation, and to rest in the knowledge that He is in control. With a sound mind, we can think clearly, make wise decisions, and trust that God is guiding our steps. Deliverance from fear means that we don't have to be controlled by anxiety, by doubts, or by the "what-ifs" of life. Instead, we can live with courage, peace, and confidence, knowing that God has given us all we need to overcome fear. He has given us power to face every challenge, love to conquer every fear, and a sound mind to stay steady and calm. With these gifts, we can walk forward in faith, free from fear, knowing that God is with us every step of the way, holding us, guiding us, and delivering us into His perfect peace.

Chapter 10 - Divine Strength

In Isaiah 40:29, we find a promise that reaches out to everyone who has ever felt weak, worn down, or weary: "He giveth power to the faint; and to them that have no might he increaseth strength." This verse speaks of Divine Strength—a gift that comes directly from God to those who feel they have reached the end of their own strength. There are moments in life when we all feel like we just can't go on. Times when the burdens we carry feel too heavy, when the trials we face seem too great, and when our own energy, hope, or resilience feels drained. It's in these moments that God's divine strength becomes our lifeline. God, who knows us better than we know ourselves, sees our exhaustion, our struggles, and our desire to give up, and He steps in to provide the strength we cannot find within ourselves. His power is perfect, limitless, and unwavering. Unlike our own strength, which fades and falters, God's strength is eternal, and He gives it generously to all who ask. When we are faint, when we feel like we're at the end of our rope, God doesn't just give us a small measure of strength—He pours it into us abundantly, giving us power that lifts us up and renews our spirit. His strength is not just a temporary boost; it is an unbreakable foundation that supports us, carries us, and enables us to face every challenge with courage. God's divine strength is a reminder that we don't have to do it all alone. We are not meant to rely solely on our own might or abilities, for we have a loving Father who is ready to empower us and strengthen us in ways we never imagined. This divine strength is what keeps us going in the darkest nights and through the fiercest storms. It allows us to rise when we have fallen, to push forward when we feel stuck, and to keep believing when hope feels far away. God's strength fills the gaps in our weakness, making us strong in Him even when we feel completely broken. He increases our might, not by asking us to be more than we are, but by filling us with His Spirit and His power. We may be faint, but He is never weary, and His strength becomes our own. This strength transforms us, giving us the endurance to press on, the resilience to overcome, and the peace to rest in His presence. With God's strength, we can do what we thought was impossible. His strength is a source of hope, reminding us that we are never alone, that we are never without help, and that, through Him, we have all we need to stand firm and move forward. His strength is more than just power—it is a gift of love, a promise that He will always be with us, helping us through every trial, lifting us through every hardship, and carrying us through every difficulty. His strength is constant, dependable, and always available, and in Him, we find the power to live boldly, joyfully, and confidently, no matter what life may bring. God's divine strength is ours, a gift that transforms our weakness into His strength and enables us to face every day with hope and courage.

Chapter 11 - Dwelling in His Presence

In Psalm 91:1, we encounter the comforting and powerful promise, "He that dwelleth in the secret place of the most High shall abide under the shadow of the Almighty." This verse speaks to the beauty and safety of Dwelling in His Presence—a place of peace, strength, and unshakable security that is found when we choose to stay close to God. Dwelling in God's presence means living in the constant awareness of His nearness, His love, and His protection. It is a promise that those who seek Him, who draw near to Him, and who trust in His strength will find a refuge that is unlike any other. God's presence is a shelter from life's storms, a hiding place where we are shielded from fear, worry, and danger. When we dwell in the "secret place" with Him, we are not only protected but deeply loved, cared for, and valued. This secret place is not a physical location; it is a spiritual state of being fully connected to our Creator, where our hearts rest in His grace and are covered by His mercy. To dwell in His presence is to be covered by His shadow, a constant reminder that He is always with us, walking beside us, going before us, and surrounding us with His love. Under His shadow, we find peace that the world cannot give, strength that the world cannot understand, and joy that cannot be taken away. Even when life feels overwhelming, even when fear or doubt tries to creep in, we have this assurance: that we are safe under the shadow of the Almighty. He is our fortress, our defender, and our unmovable rock. Dwelling in His presence means that we are never alone; God is our constant companion, listening to our prayers, calming our fears, and reminding us that we are His. In His presence, we find healing for our wounds, comfort for our sorrows, and strength to face each day with courage. There, in the secret place, we are known fully and loved deeply. God doesn't ask us to be perfect to come into His presence; He invites us as we are, with all our struggles, our weaknesses, and our fears. And when we come to Him, He doesn't just meet us—He embraces us, filling us with His peace and

His power. Dwelling in His presence changes us; it shapes our hearts to reflect His love and strengthens our faith to trust in His goodness. We begin to see life differently, not because our circumstances have changed, but because we know that God is with us. He holds us close, guards our hearts, and gives us the courage to keep going. This closeness with God is a relationship built on trust, love, and surrender. As we dwell in His presence, we let go of our fears and burdens, handing them over to the One who can carry them. He becomes our source of hope, our joy, and our purpose. We no longer have to search for peace or try to protect ourselves, for God Himself becomes our shield, our comfort, and our guide. In His presence, we find the fulfillment our souls long for, the peace our minds crave, and the love our hearts desperately need. We can live each day with confidence, knowing that we are covered by His shadow and safe in His embrace. Dwelling in His presence is the greatest gift, a sanctuary where we are never alone, never abandoned, and always surrounded by the unbreakable love of the Almighty.

Chapter 12 - Delight in the Lord

In Psalm 37:4, we are invited into a beautiful and joyful relationship with God: "Delight thyself also in the LORD; and he shall give thee the desires of thine heart." This verse speaks to the incredible blessing of Delight in the Lord—a deep and genuine joy found in knowing, loving, and trusting God with all our heart. To delight in the Lord is to find our greatest happiness in Him, to savor the moments we spend in His presence, and to cherish His words, His promises, and His ways above all else. It's more than just a fleeting feeling; it's a choice to set our hearts on Him, to find peace in His love, and to be grateful for His goodness every day. When we delight in the Lord, we draw close to Him, letting go of our worries, our fears, and even our own plans, because we trust that His plans are greater than ours. This delight is a celebration of who God is—His kindness, His wisdom, His power, and His never-ending love for us. In delighting in Him, we allow our desires to be shaped and aligned with His perfect will. As we focus on His goodness, our hearts start to change, and we begin to want what He wants for us. We start to desire what will bring Him glory and what will bring us closer to Him. And in this beautiful exchange, God doesn't just ignore our desires; He promises to fulfill them in ways we could never imagine. He knows the deepest longings of our hearts, the dreams we hold close, and the hopes we sometimes dare not speak aloud, and when we delight in Him, He faithfully gives us what is best. This doesn't mean that He always gives us exactly what we think we want, but rather that He gives us the very best for our lives, often in ways that far exceed our expectations. Our delight in the Lord transforms how we see life; it fills us with joy even in difficult times because our happiness is rooted in Him, not in our circumstances. He becomes our source of peace, our fountain of joy, and our deepest satisfaction. When we find our delight in God, we are not left wanting, because He is enough, and He fills every empty place in our hearts.

This delight leads us to worship Him more fully, to serve others with love, and to live each day with gratitude and faith. It's a joy that overflows, touching everyone around us, as we live as reflections of His love and light. When we delight in the Lord, life becomes a journey of discovering His goodness more and more each day, and we come to see that every blessing, every moment of peace, and every fulfilled desire is a gift from His loving hand. Our delight in God is a response to His love for us, a love so deep and true that it transforms us from the inside out. As we place our trust in Him, as we delight in His presence, and as we let Him guide our desires, we find a life filled with joy, purpose, and peace, knowing that the desires of our hearts are safe in His hands, and that He is always faithful to provide for His children.

Chapter 13 - Dominion Over Sin

In Romans 6:14, we are given one of the most powerful promises about freedom and victory, "For sin shall not have dominion over you: for ye are not under the law, but under grace." This verse speaks to the life-changing gift of Dominion Over Sin that we receive through Jesus Christ. It means that sin, with all its temptations and traps, no longer has control over us; we are free from its power because of God's amazing grace. Sin once ruled our lives, making us feel trapped in cycles of wrong choices, guilt, and regret. It would pull us down, keeping us from living the life God intended. But now, through the sacrifice of Jesus, sin no longer has dominion over us. We are no longer slaves to our mistakes, weaknesses, or the habits we thought we could never overcome. Grace has stepped in, offering us a new way to live—a way of freedom, hope, and strength. Grace is the love of God reaching out to us, picking us up, and helping us live beyond our old ways. We do not have to earn this grace; it is a gift, freely given because God loves us so much. He knew we could not break free on our own, so He sent Jesus to conquer sin and give us this victory. Living under grace means we have God's help, His forgiveness, and His power to say "no" to sin and "yes" to a life that honors Him. It doesn't mean we will never struggle, but it does mean that sin's control over us is broken. Each time we face temptation, we can rely on God's strength, knowing He has already made a way for us to overcome. This dominion over sin brings peace, because we know our failures do not define us anymore; God's grace does. Our identity is no longer tied to our past mistakes but to the freedom Christ has given us. When we stumble, we can get back up, knowing His grace is there to forgive us, guide us, and empower us. We are new creations, no longer bound by the chains of sin, but set free to live with purpose and joy. This freedom changes how we see ourselves and how we live each day. Sin may try to pull us back, but it cannot overpower the grace that now defines us. God's grace is stronger than any sin, any failure, and any regret, and it reminds us daily that we are loved and valued. Dominion over sin is not about our strength but about God's victory, which He shares with us. As we live under grace, we experience the joy of knowing that sin does not control our destiny—God's love does. His grace gives us the courage to live boldly, to choose righteousness, and to walk in the freedom He designed for us. It is a freedom that fills us with hope, peace, and gratitude, knowing that God's grace is always enough and that we are forever free in Him.

Chapter 14 - Divine Comfort

In 2 Corinthians 1:3, we read a powerful truth about God's heart for us: "Blessed be God, even the Father of our Lord Jesus Christ, the Father of mercies, and the God of all comfort." This verse reveals God as the Divine Comforter, the One who reaches into our deepest pain, sorrow, and struggles, surrounding us with a peace and love that only He can give. He is not just a distant Creator; He is a loving Father who knows our weaknesses, feels our pain, and offers us comfort in every situation. No matter what we face—whether it's loss, disappointment, fear, or sadness—God's comfort is always available to us, steady and unshakable. Life can sometimes bring moments that feel overwhelming, where the burdens seem too heavy and the struggles too intense. Yet, in those times, God's comfort becomes our anchor, grounding us in His mercy and wrapping us in His love. This comfort is more than a feeling; it's the strength He provides, the peace that calms our anxieties, and the gentle reminder that we are never alone. When we feel broken, God's comfort is like a healing balm, touching every wound and assuring us that He is with us, carrying us when we are weak and guiding us through every storm. As the "Father of mercies," His compassion is endless—He sees our tears, hears our cries, and understands our needs even when words fail. His comfort doesn't mean that we will never face hardships, but it means that we have a refuge in Him, a safe place where we can rest, find hope, and be renewed. God's comfort is constant, present in the quiet moments of prayer, in the strength He gives us to keep going, and in the promises He has made to never leave nor forsake us. Each time we turn to Him, we are met with open arms and a heart that overflows with mercy and kindness. His comfort reaches into the very depths of our soul, reminding us that we are cherished, protected, and loved beyond measure. No trial or sorrow can take away His comforting presence, for He is the God of all comfort, the One who fills us with peace when nothing else can.

When we are weak, He becomes our strength; when we are lost, He is our guide; and when we are weary, He renews our spirit. In His comfort, we find a love that never fails, a mercy that never runs dry, and a hope that lights our way through even the darkest nights. His comfort is a gift, a divine assurance that in Him, we are safe, held, and understood. As we rest in His comfort, we find the courage to face each day, knowing that we are never alone and that our Heavenly Father walks with us, sustaining us, healing us, and comforting us with a love that is eternal and unbreakable.

Chapter 15 - Deliverance from Trials

In Psalm 34:19, we are given a powerful promise of hope and strength: "Many are the afflictions of the righteous: but the LORD delivereth him out of them all." This verse speaks of the Deliverance from Trials that God provides for those who trust in Him. Life is filled with challenges, sorrows, and unexpected trials that test our faith and sometimes shake us to our core. We face situations that seem too difficult to handle, struggles that feel never-ending, and battles that leave us feeling exhausted and alone. But here in this verse, God promises that He will not leave us in our troubles; He will deliver us out of every single one. For the righteous, those who seek to follow God, trials are a part of the journey, yet they are never faced alone. God sees every tear, every pain, and every struggle, and He steps into each one with us, offering His strength, His peace, and His deliverance. When we feel overwhelmed, He is our rock, our fortress, and our deliverer, standing with us and fighting for us. His deliverance is not just about removing us from difficult situations; it's about carrying us through them, strengthening us, and helping us grow in faith. Even when it seems like there's no way out, God is working behind the scenes, opening doors, breaking down walls, and making a way where there seems to be none. His deliverance means that no matter how many trials we face, we can have confidence that God will see us through every one of them. He knows exactly what we need and when we need it, and He is faithful to provide. This doesn't mean we won't face hardships, but it means that every hardship has a purpose and a promise—that God will bring us through to the other side. In times of trial, His presence is our comfort, His Word is our guide, and His love is our shield. He reminds us that we are never alone, for He walks with us, holding our hand and lifting our spirit. When our strength is gone, He becomes our strength; when our hope fades, He renews it; and when we feel like we can't go on, He carries us. God's deliverance is a reminder of His power and His love, a promise that we are never abandoned in our trials. He is the God who parts seas, who brings light into the darkest places, and who turns our mourning into joy. With each trial we face, we learn to rely more on Him, to trust His timing, and to find peace in His presence. Every deliverance becomes a testimony of His goodness, a story of His faithfulness, and a reminder that He is always with us. As we hold onto this promise, we can face every trial with courage, knowing that no matter how great the struggle, God's deliverance is greater.

Chapter 16 - Discipline of the Lord

In Hebrews 12:6, we find a profound truth that may at first seem difficult to understand but is rooted in deep love: "For whom the Lord loveth he chasteneth, and scourgeth every son whom he receiveth." This verse reveals the Discipline of the Lord, a discipline that is not about punishment, but about love, guidance, and growth. Just as a loving parent corrects a child to keep them safe and to help them grow, God, our Heavenly Father, disciplines us out of love. His discipline is not a sign of His anger or rejection; rather, it is evidence that He cares for us deeply and wants the best for us. When God disciplines us, He is shaping our character, teaching us right from wrong, and helping us to become more like Him. This discipline is a refining process that strengthens our faith, builds our patience, and fills us with wisdom. Though it may be uncomfortable or challenging, God's discipline is always for our good, and it is meant to bring us closer to Him. He knows our weaknesses, our struggles, and the areas where we need to grow, and in His love, He guides us through each one. The discipline of the Lord may come in the form of conviction, where He gently shows us our mistakes, or it may be through difficult circumstances that teach us reliance on Him. Whatever form it takes, we can trust that His discipline is always guided by His love and purpose. It's His way of saying, "I love you too much to let you stay the same." In these moments, God's discipline is drawing us away from harmful paths and bringing us into a life that reflects His holiness and goodness. Even when it's hard to understand, we can find comfort in knowing that God's discipline is preparing us for something greater. He is not content to leave us where we are; He is always working to make us better, stronger, and more faithful. Just as gold is refined in fire, so are we refined through God's loving discipline, becoming more valuable, more resilient, and more aligned with His will. His discipline is a sign of our belonging to Him, a mark of His commitment to us as His children. It assures us that He is invested in our lives and that He will never give up on us. Each time He disciplines us, He is reminding us of His love and His desire for us to grow in righteousness. Though discipline may be hard, it brings forth a harvest of peace, joy, and a closer relationship with God. We can trust that His hand is gentle and His intentions are pure, for He disciplines us not to harm us but to heal us, to guide us, and to bring us to a place of blessing.

Chapter 17 - Drawn Near to God

"Draw nigh to God, and he will draw nigh to you" (James 4:8) is a verse that offers one of the most beautiful invitations and promises from God. It shows the very heart of God's desire to be close to each of us, revealing the power, peace, and joy that come from being Drawn Near to God. These simple words encourage us to take that first step toward Him, assuring us that God is not distant or unreachable. Instead, He longs for a deep and personal connection with every heart that genuinely seeks Him. This invitation isn't exclusive to a select few—it is for everyone, no matter who we are, where we've been, or what we've done. The promise is open to each of us: if we take even the smallest step in His direction, God moves closer to us, meeting us with open arms filled with love, forgiveness, and grace.

To draw near to God means choosing to open our hearts to Him, sharing our fears, our joys, our dreams, and our struggles with the One who cares for us more deeply than we can comprehend. It means spending time with Him in prayer, reading His Word, and quieting our busy thoughts to listen for His voice. We do not need to be perfect or to have our lives fully together to come near to God. All He asks is that we come as we are, with open hearts, seeking His presence. And when we do, we find that His love surrounds us like a warm embrace, providing comfort, peace, and healing to our souls.

There is something incredibly comforting about knowing that the Creator of the universe wants to be close to us, to be involved in the details of our lives, and to walk with us through every high and low. This closeness with God fills the empty spaces in our hearts, bringing a joy and contentment that the world cannot provide. When we draw near to Him, we experience a unique kind of peace—a peace that calms our anxieties and gives us strength in our weakest moments. In His presence, we find a refuge from life's storms, a place where we are loved unconditionally, and a safe space where we can rest and renew.

Drawing near to God is a journey that transforms us. As we spend time in His presence, we begin to see the world through His eyes. We become more compassionate, more patient, and more forgiving, reflecting the love that we receive from Him. His love fills us, shaping our character and helping us to become more like Him. Each step we take toward God brings us into a deeper understanding of who He is and who He created us to be. We come to realize that in His presence, we are not just loved; we are cherished. We are not just known; we are understood deeply and completely.

In drawing near to God, we also find healing for our hurts, comfort for our sorrows, and hope for our future. Life can be full of challenges and hardships that leave us feeling broken or lost, but when we seek God's presence, He is there to lift us up and to mend what is broken. His nearness reminds us that we are never alone, that there is no pain too great, no wound too deep, that His love cannot heal. He listens to every prayer, understands every sigh, and knows every tear that falls. He is with us in the moments of joy and in the moments of sorrow, standing by our side as a faithful friend and loving Father.

When we choose to draw near to God, we begin to experience the joy of His guidance, the warmth of His compassion, and the comfort of His unwavering support. His wisdom becomes our guide, helping us make choices that honor Him and lead to a life filled with purpose and meaning. His voice becomes our comfort in times of distress, and His promises become the anchor for our soul. The more we draw near to Him, the more we realize that His ways are better than ours and that His plans for us are full of hope and goodness.

The journey of drawing near to God is also one of surrender. It's about letting go of the things that hold us back, the fears that keep us distant, and the doubts that cloud our view of His love. As we come closer to Him, we find the courage to let go of our worries, to release our burdens, and to place our trust fully in Him. We learn that we don't have to carry the weight of the world on our shoulders because God is more than able to handle it. He invites us to cast our cares upon Him, promising that He will sustain us and give us rest.

This promise that God will draw near to us as we draw near to Him is a reminder that we are never truly alone. Even in the quiet moments when we may feel forgotten or unseen, God is there, closer than our own breath, surrounding us with His presence. He walks with us through every season of life, guiding us when we are lost, comforting us when we are hurting, and rejoicing with us in times of gladness. His closeness brings a sense of belonging, a feeling that we are part of something greater than ourselves. In His presence, we find the fulfillment our souls long for, the peace our hearts crave, and the love our spirits desperately need.

God's promise to draw near to us is not a fleeting or conditional offer. It is a constant invitation, always open, and always available. No matter how far we may feel from Him, no matter how many mistakes we've made, He is always ready to welcome us back with open arms. His love is patient and kind, waiting for us to take that step toward Him. Every time we draw near, we are met with grace, mercy, and forgiveness. He doesn't hold our past against us or keep a record of our wrongs. Instead, He sees us as His beloved children, worthy of His love, and invites us into a relationship that fills us with peace and purpose.

As we draw near to God, we discover a strength that we didn't know we had. We find that, through Him, we can face life's challenges with courage and resilience. His presence empowers us, giving us the confidence to move forward even when the path seems uncertain. He stands beside us, encouraging us and reminding us that we are never fighting alone. With God by our side, we have the strength to overcome obstacles, the wisdom to navigate difficulties, and the peace to handle whatever comes our way.

The closer we draw to God, the more we come to understand His character and His heart for us. We see His kindness in the way He provides for our needs, His faithfulness in the way He keeps His promises, and His grace in the way He forgives our sins. Each moment spent in His presence reveals more of His beauty and His goodness, drawing us into a deeper relationship with Him. We come to know God not just as a distant Creator but as a loving Father, a faithful friend, and a wise guide.

This closeness with God transforms not only our relationship with Him but also our relationships with others. When we are filled with His love, we are able to love others more deeply, forgive more easily, and show compassion more freely. His love fills us to the point that it overflows, touching everyone around us. As we draw near to God, we become a reflection of His love and light in the world, bringing hope and encouragement to those around us.

In God's presence, we find rest for our weary souls and joy that cannot be taken away. The journey of drawing near to Him is a journey of discovery—discovering who He is, who we are in Him, and the incredible love

He has for us. It is a journey that leads us into a life filled with purpose, peace, and endless joy. The more we seek Him, the more we find that His presence is everything we need, filling every empty place in our hearts and providing a love that never fails.

God's invitation to draw near is a gift, an opportunity to experience a relationship with Him that is deep, real, and life-changing. It's a promise that, no matter where we are or what we're going through, He is always there, ready to meet us, to comfort us, and to draw us into His love. This relationship with God is the foundation for a life of faith, hope, and joy. It's a relationship that sustains us, guides us, and brings us a peace that the world cannot give. And as we continue to draw near to Him, we are transformed, becoming more like Christ, filled with His love, His wisdom, and His grace.

In every season of life, whether in times of joy or sorrow, peace or struggle, we have the assurance that God is with us. His promise to draw near to us is a source of hope, a reminder that we are not alone, and a call to experience His love in a deeper, more meaningful way. This journey of drawing near is a journey into the heart of God, where we find a love that is patient, kind, and unwavering. It's a journey that leads us into a life of purpose and fulfillment, where we are known, loved, and cherished by the Creator of the universe.

As we take each step toward God, we can rest in the confidence that He will always be there to meet us, to hold us, and to guide us. His presence is our refuge, His love is our strength, and His grace is our salvation. To draw near to God is to find everything we have been searching for—a love that completes us, a peace that calms us, and a joy that fills our hearts. This is the promise of James 4:8, and it is a promise that we can hold onto every day of our lives, knowing that, as we draw near to God, He will draw near to us, filling us with His presence, His love, and His unending grace.

Chapter 18 - Dependence on His Faithfulness

In 1 Thessalonians 5:24, we find a beautiful assurance that reaches straight to the heart: "Faithful is he that calleth you, who also will do it." This verse speaks of our Dependence on His Faithfulness, a faithfulness so complete, so unwavering, and so deep that it becomes the very foundation on which we can stand, no matter what life brings. When we truly grasp the meaning of God's faithfulness, it changes everything about how we live and how we see ourselves. It's a promise that we can rely on completely because it comes from God Himself, who never changes, never falters, and never turns back on His word. To say that God is faithful means that He keeps every promise, fulfills every word, and always does what He says He will do. He isn't like people who may sometimes fail us or like situations that can change in an instant; His faithfulness is unchanging and true. This promise tells us that whatever God calls us to, He will carry it through. When He gives us a purpose, a task, or a dream, He doesn't expect us to do it all on our own. Instead, He stays with us, walking beside us, guiding our steps, and giving us strength when ours runs out.

God's faithfulness is not just a comforting idea; it is a reality that we can experience in every season of our lives. When He calls us, He equips us, providing the wisdom, courage, and resources we need to accomplish what He has placed before us. Even when we feel weak, uncertain, or inadequate, His faithfulness fills every gap in our abilities, reminding us that we don't have to rely on our own strength alone. God's faithfulness means that He will finish what He begins in us. It assures us that, though we may feel lost or unsure, He sees the whole picture and is guiding us toward His perfect plan. This promise of faithfulness allows us to breathe easy, knowing that God's plan for us is solid and unshakable. We don't have to live in fear of failure because, when God calls us, He also empowers us to accomplish it. Dependence on His faithfulness is a steadying truth in a world that is often chaotic and uncertain.

Life can be filled with challenges, disappointments, and even moments that test our deepest faith. But in these times, God's faithfulness remains our anchor, holding us steady in the storm and giving us the courage to keep going. His faithfulness means that He never leaves us on our own to figure things out. Instead, He is actively involved in every step of our journey, guiding us with His wisdom, protecting us with His love, and strengthening us with His power.

Relying on God's faithfulness means placing our trust fully in Him, knowing that He is working everything out according to His perfect will. We may not always understand why things happen the way they do, but we can be sure that God's plan is always for our good. His faithfulness assures us that He is with us through every high and low, every joy and sorrow, and every success and failure. Even when our faith wavers, God's faithfulness never does. He is the rock on which we stand, a safe place where we can rest, knowing that He is in control. This dependence on God's faithfulness allows us to face each day with peace, knowing that we are held in His hands, protected by His promises, and secure in His love. His faithfulness isn't something we have to earn or deserve; it is a gift that He gives freely to those who trust in Him. Even when we stumble or fall short, God remains faithful, picking us up, forgiving us, and helping us move forward.

God's faithfulness is what makes it possible for us to step out in courage, even when the road ahead is uncertain. Because He is faithful, we can take risks, dream big, and live boldly, knowing that He will never fail us. He goes before us, preparing the way, and walks beside us, providing strength and guidance. This promise means that we don't have to live in fear or worry about the future. No matter what challenges come our way, we can rely on God to be there, faithfully guiding us, supporting us, and helping us to accomplish His purposes. His faithfulness is not dependent on our actions; it is rooted in His character. He is faithful because it is who He is. This faithfulness is not just a comforting thought—it is a truth that we can lean on, a foundation that can never be shaken.

When we depend on God's faithfulness, we are freed from the weight of trying to control everything ourselves. We don't have to rely solely on our own abilities, wisdom, or resources; we can rest, knowing that God is more than able to handle every challenge and meet every need. His faithfulness means that He is always working for our good, even in ways we cannot see. Sometimes life takes unexpected turns, or we face trials that we never anticipated, but in every situation, God is faithful. He is there in the moments of joy and celebration, and He is there in the seasons of sorrow and struggle. His faithfulness assures us that we are never alone, that we are always loved, and that we have a purpose that is guided by His perfect plan.

This dependence on God's faithfulness also brings peace. Knowing that God will never leave us or forsake us, we can let go of fear and trust Him fully. His faithfulness is our anchor in the storm, our light in the darkness, and our hope when life feels overwhelming. He is the God who parts the seas, who moves mountains, and who brings life from places of despair. His faithfulness reminds us that no matter how difficult our path may seem, God is with us, helping us, strengthening us, and ensuring that we are never abandoned. When we place our trust in Him, we find a peace that surpasses all understanding, a peace that calms our fears and gives us confidence to face each day.

God's faithfulness is also the reason we can hope. It assures us that our lives are not left to chance or luck but are carefully held in the hands of a loving Creator who has a good and perfect plan for us. His faithfulness means that every promise He has made will come to pass, that every word He has spoken is true, and that every purpose He has for us will be fulfilled. This hope gives us strength to persevere, to keep moving forward, and to believe that the best is yet to come. His faithfulness assures us that He is always working on our behalf, that He is always listening to our prayers, and that He is always guiding us according to His perfect will.

When we depend on God's faithfulness, we also find freedom. Freedom from worry, freedom from fear, and freedom from the pressures of trying to do it all on our own. His faithfulness reminds us that we don't have to have all the answers, because we know the One who does. It gives us the courage to step out in faith, knowing that God is with us and that He will never leave us. This freedom allows us to live each day with joy, knowing that we are loved, cared for, and guided by a faithful God who holds our future in His hands.

God's faithfulness is a constant source of comfort and strength. When life feels uncertain or overwhelming, His faithfulness is there to remind us that we are never alone. He is our provider, our protector, and our guide, faithfully leading us and taking care of every need. His faithfulness assures us that no matter what challenges we face, He is with us, giving us strength, courage, and peace. We can face each day with confidence, knowing that God's faithfulness is unchanging and that His love for us is everlasting.

Dependence on God's faithfulness is a journey of trust, a walk of faith that brings us closer to Him each day. As we learn to rely on His faithfulness, we find that He is more than enough for every situation, every challenge, and every moment of our lives. He is the God who keeps His promises, who finishes what He starts, and who loves us with a love that is constant and true. His faithfulness is our foundation, our hope, and our strength, allowing us to live each day with peace, joy, and confidence, knowing that we are in the hands of a faithful God who will never let us go.

Chapter 19 - Divine Encouragement

In Isaiah 41:10, we receive one of the most beautiful and reassuring promises from God: "Fear thou not; for I am with thee: be not dismayed; for I am thy God." This verse is all about Divine Encouragement, a promise that fills our hearts with courage, hope, and strength. It is a reminder that no matter what we face in life, we do not have to be afraid or discouraged, because God Himself is with us every step of the way. When fears creep in, when worries weigh us down, and when life feels overwhelming, these words remind us that we are not alone. God, the Creator of the universe, is by our side, watching over us, holding us up, and guiding us through every storm. He says, "Fear thou not," because He knows that fear can paralyze us, make us feel small, and keep us from stepping into the purpose He has for us. But with His presence, we have a source of strength greater than anything we can face. God's encouragement is not just words; it is His promise to be with us, to be our shield, our rock, and our fortress. To "be not dismayed" means that even in moments of confusion, heartbreak, or disappointment, we can hold onto the truth that God is in control and that He has a good plan for our lives. He knows our struggles, our battles, and our doubts, and He promises to be our constant source of comfort and support. Divine encouragement means that God's presence gives us the strength to keep going, the peace to rest in His love, and the courage to face each day with faith. We may not have all the answers, but we know the One who does, and His promise to be our God means that He is not just watching from afar—He is actively involved in our lives, caring for us, providing for us, and leading us. This encouragement from God fills us with a deep sense of peace, knowing that nothing we face is too big for Him, that no problem is beyond His power, and that no fear is greater than His love. In times of weakness, He becomes our strength; in times of sorrow, He is our comfort; and in times of doubt, He is our assurance. With God by our side, we have everything we need to overcome every challenge, to rise above every obstacle, and to live with confidence and joy. His encouragement is like a light that shines in the darkness, guiding us, reassuring us, and reminding us that we are deeply loved and never alone. This promise gives us the courage to live boldly, to trust deeply, and to rest in the unfailing love of a God who says, "I am with thee," and who will never leave nor forsake us.

Chapter 20 - Diligent Faith

In Hebrews 11:6, we find a truth that stirs our hearts and calls us to a deeper commitment: "But without faith it is impossible to please him... he is a rewarder of them that diligently seek him." This verse speaks to the importance of Diligent Faith—a faith that goes beyond belief alone and calls us to seek God earnestly, faithfully, and wholeheartedly. Diligent faith is not passive; it is active, full of life and persistence. It's the kind of faith that doesn't just believe God exists but trusts that He is good, loving, and deeply involved in our lives. Diligent faith means seeking God in every season, through every high and low, knowing that our efforts to know Him and walk with Him are not in vain. This kind of faith doesn't give up, even when things are difficult or when we face challenges that seem overwhelming. Instead, diligent faith presses on, trusting that God will come through, because He has promised to reward those who earnestly seek Him. Seeking God with diligence means spending time in prayer, pouring out our hearts to Him, listening for His guidance, and holding onto His promises even when the answers aren't clear. It means opening His Word, learning His truth, and letting it shape our hearts, minds, and lives. God is pleased with this kind of faith because it shows that we believe in His goodness and are willing to trust Him, no matter what. This diligent faith is like a journey—a journey that brings us closer to God, that strengthens our spirits, and that fills us with hope and joy. God is not distant or disinterested; He is right here with us, inviting us to seek Him, to know Him, and to walk with Him each day. Diligent faith reminds us that God rewards those who seek Him not just with material blessings, but with the gift of His presence, His peace, and His love. He fills our hearts with strength and our minds with wisdom, helping us face each day with courage and purpose. When we diligently seek God, we find that He meets us right where we are, ready to listen, to comfort, and to guide. Our faith becomes a source of joy, a wellspring of peace, and a foundation of strength that cannot be shaken. Diligent faith is pleasing to God because it honors Him, showing that we trust in His promises and that we know He is faithful. It is a faith that draws us close to God, helping us to live each day in the light of His love and to walk confidently in the assurance that He is with us. This promise of diligent faith is a call to live with purpose, to seek God above all else, and to experience the joy of knowing Him deeply. With diligent faith, we are never alone, for God rewards us with His presence, His peace, and His guidance, giving us everything we need to live a life that honors Him and reflects His love.

Chapter 21 - Defense Against Evil

In Ephesians 6:11, we are given a powerful command and a source of strength: "Put on the whole armour of God, that ye may be able to stand against the wiles of the devil." This verse calls us to prepare ourselves with the Defense Against Evil that only God can provide, equipping us for the spiritual battles we face in life. Every day, we are surrounded by challenges, temptations, and unseen forces that seek to pull us away from God's truth and purpose for us. The world can be full of darkness, doubt, and lies that try to weaken our faith or make us lose hope. But God, knowing our struggles, has not left us defenseless. He offers us His armor—a full, divine protection that covers every part of who we are. Putting on the armor of God means choosing to stand in His strength, relying not on our own abilities but on the mighty power of the Lord. This armor, crafted by God, includes truth, righteousness, the gospel of peace, faith, salvation, and the Word of God—each piece designed to protect, guide, and strengthen us in our fight against evil. The armor of truth helps us to see through lies and stand firm in what is real and godly. The breastplate of righteousness shields our hearts, reminding us to live in ways that honor God and reflect His love. The gospel of peace grounds us, giving us stability and purpose, so that we may walk confidently in God's promises. The shield of faith is our defense against doubt, fear, and temptation, helping us to trust in God even when life feels uncertain. The helmet of salvation protects our minds, filling us with the knowledge of who we are in Christ—saved, loved, and redeemed. And the sword of the Spirit, which is the Word of God, is our weapon against the lies and deceptions that try to lead us astray. With this armor, we are prepared to face anything that comes our way, knowing that God Himself is with us, fighting for us, and providing everything we need to stand strong. The armor of God is not something we wear just once; it's something we put on daily, choosing to trust in His protection, His wisdom, and His guidance. In this armor, we find courage, hope, and the assurance that we are never alone. God's armor gives us the strength to stand firm, even when the battle feels tough, and to hold on to His promises, knowing that His power is greater than anything we face. This armor is God's gift to us, a reminder that He is our defender, our refuge, and our protector, and that in Him, we have the ultimate victory.

Chapter 22 - Divine Healing

In Psalm 103:3, we find a beautiful and comforting promise from God: "Who forgiveth all thine iniquities; who healeth all thy diseases." This verse reminds us of the profound power of Divine Healing, revealing God as the ultimate Healer, the One who not only forgives our sins but also brings healing to every area of our lives. His healing is a gift that touches us deeply, going beyond physical ailments to reach into our hearts, minds, and spirits, offering us peace, hope, and strength. Divine healing is God's way of showing us His love and compassion. When we feel broken, weak, or worn down by life, God is there, ready to heal us, to lift us up, and to make us whole. His healing is perfect and complete, covering every wound, every scar, and every hurt, whether seen or unseen. Whether it's a sickness, a struggle, or a hidden pain, God's healing brings us relief, restoration, and a renewed sense of peace. He is the God who sees our silent tears, who hears our unspoken prayers, and who understands the depths of our pain. In those moments when we feel alone or overwhelmed, His healing presence fills us with comfort, reassuring us that we are held in His loving arms.

God's healing isn't limited to the physical body; it reaches into our deepest sorrows, our fears, and our doubts, bringing light into the darkest parts of our lives. It's a healing that restores our joy, gives us peace, and strengthens our faith. When we come to Him, whether in moments of sickness, weariness, or despair, He meets us with open arms, ready to heal and to comfort. His forgiveness removes the guilt and shame that can weigh on our hearts, lifting our spirits and giving us a fresh start. He heals not only our diseases but our wounds, our brokenness, and our insecurities. Divine healing means we don't have to carry our burdens alone; God is with us, taking on our struggles and giving us the strength to overcome them. We don't have to be perfect or do anything special to receive His healing; it is a gift freely given to us because He loves us so deeply.

In His presence, we find a place of refuge and safety, where healing takes root and begins to transform us from the inside out.

God's healing is a reminder that we are never alone, that we are cherished, and that we are cared for. He walks with us through every trial, comforting us, strengthening us, and guiding us toward wholeness. His healing power renews us, giving us the courage to face each day with hope and the assurance that He is in control. This divine healing journey brings us closer to God, helping us to trust in His love and to rely on His strength. As we experience His healing, we learn that His grace is enough, that His mercy is endless, and that His love will never fail us. We come to see that in every moment of weakness, God's power is made perfect, and His healing presence is with us, renewing us, restoring us, and giving us life.

Chapter 23 - Destined for Eternity

In John 14:2, Jesus offers one of the most comforting promises we could ever receive: "In my Father's house are many mansions... I go to prepare a place for you." These words remind us that we are Destined for Eternity—that God has prepared a place for us in heaven, a perfect home where we will dwell with Him forever. This promise fills our hearts with hope, reminding us that this world, with all its struggles, pains, and temporary joys, is not our final destination. Jesus, our Savior, left heaven and came to earth to redeem us, to make a way for us to have eternal life with Him. And now, He has returned to His Father to prepare a place for each of us, a place where there is no sorrow, no pain, and no death—only peace, love, and endless joy. To think that Jesus, the King of kings, personally prepares a place for us shows us just how deeply loved we are. We are not an afterthought or just another face in a crowd; we are individually cherished and known by God, who longs to have us with Him forever. This promise of eternity is a reminder that we are more than just flesh and bone; we are souls created with purpose, souls that are destined to live on even after our time on earth comes to an end. Each day we live brings us one step closer to the day when we will finally see Him face to face, when all the struggles of this life will fade away, and we will stand in the presence of His glory. Jesus assures us that there are "many mansions" in His Father's house, meaning that heaven has room for all who believe in Him. There is a place for everyone who trusts in Him, a place tailored with love, filled with peace, and radiant with the glory of God. In this eternal home, we will experience love like never before, a love that is pure, whole, and perfect. There will be no more tears, no more fear, and no more separation from our Creator. This promise gives us hope in our darkest moments, reminding us that the pains of this world are only temporary, and that a beautiful, eternal home awaits us. It encourages us to live with purpose, to hold onto our faith, and to remember that our journey here is only a small part of the story. We are not just living for today; we are living with eternity in mind, with a future that is secure in Christ. This knowledge that we are destined for eternity allows us to face life's challenges with peace, knowing that nothing can take away the place that Jesus has prepared for us. It's a promise that speaks to our deepest longings, our desire to belong, to be loved, and to be at peace. In heaven, every longing of our hearts will be fulfilled, every question answered, and every tear wiped away. We will be home, forever with the One who loves us most. This promise of eternal life fills us with hope, joy, and an unshakeable assurance that our lives have meaning beyond this world. We are destined for eternity, and that truth gives us the strength to live each day in faith, knowing that Jesus has prepared a place for us in His Father's house, a place where we will dwell with Him in love, joy, and peace for all time.

Chapter 24 - Divine Wisdom

In James 1:5, we are given an amazing promise about God's readiness to guide us: "If any of you lack wisdom, let him ask of God, that giveth to all men liberally." This verse speaks of Divine Wisdom, a precious gift that comes directly from God to help us navigate life with understanding, clarity, and purpose. Divine wisdom is not like worldly knowledge; it is a deeper insight and understanding that helps us to make the right choices, to discern truth, and to follow God's path, especially in difficult times. When we lack direction, feel unsure, or face situations that are too big for us, we can turn to God, asking for His wisdom, and He promises to give it to us freely, generously, and without holding back. He does not judge us for asking; He welcomes our need for guidance and is delighted when we seek His help. God's wisdom is like a light that shines on our path, helping us to see what is right and good, leading us away from harm, and keeping us on the road that leads to His blessings. Life often presents us with complex choices, and it can be difficult to know which way to go or what decision to make, but God's wisdom is always available to us, guiding our steps and giving us peace of mind. Divine wisdom helps us to live in ways that honor Him, to speak words that build others up, and to make choices that bring us closer to His heart. It's a wisdom that brings clarity to confusion, hope to uncertainty, and strength to weakness. God's wisdom is perfect, and it is rooted in His love for us, ensuring that every piece of advice, every bit of guidance He provides, is for our good and His glory. All we have to do is ask, and He will pour out His wisdom like a river, refreshing us, enlightening us, and giving us the understanding we need to walk confidently in His will. Divine wisdom is not something we can earn or buy; it is a gift given to us by a loving Father who desires that we walk in truth and light. This wisdom is accessible to everyone, no matter who we are or what we've done. Whether we are young or old, new in faith or mature, God's wisdom is always within reach, ready to fill us and guide us in the way we should go. When we rely on His wisdom, we are spared from many mistakes, heartaches, and regrets, as He leads us along paths of righteousness. His wisdom is our shield, our guide, and our peace, helping us to face life's challenges with courage and grace. Divine wisdom gives us the insight to understand others, the patience to handle difficult situations, and the strength to overcome obstacles. It helps us to love more deeply, to live more fully, and to serve more faithfully. With God's wisdom, we are equipped to make decisions that reflect His goodness, to walk in His light, and to live lives that bring glory to His name. This wisdom transforms us, making us more like Christ, teaching us to see with God's eyes, and helping us to live with purpose and joy. In every moment of uncertainty, in every challenge we face, we can rest in the promise that if we lack wisdom, all we have to do is ask, and God will give it to us abundantly, leading us with His loving hand every step of the way.

Chapter 25 - Deliverance from Temptation

In 1 Corinthians 10:13, we are given an incredibly reassuring promise that fills us with hope and courage: "God is faithful, who will not suffer you to be tempted above that ye are able." This verse speaks to the amazing reality of Deliverance from Temptation, showing us that God understands our struggles and is actively involved in helping us overcome every challenge that tempts us. Temptation is something we all face, a powerful force that can try to pull us away from God's path, testing our hearts and our strength. But God, in His great love and wisdom, promises that He will never allow us to be tempted beyond what we can bear. He knows our limits, our weaknesses, and our needs, and He faithfully provides a way out of every temptation that we encounter. This is not just a hopeful thought; it is a guaranteed promise from our faithful God, who stands with us in every trial and temptation. When we face struggles, whether they are moments of doubt, times of fear, or times when we feel pulled toward things that we know aren't right, God is there, offering us strength, wisdom, and a clear path forward. He doesn't leave us to battle temptation on our own. Instead, He equips us, giving us His strength to stand firm, His wisdom to see the right path, and His Spirit to empower us to resist and overcome. Knowing that God will never allow us to face a temptation that is too great for us to handle brings peace to our hearts. It reminds us that we are not alone in our battles, that He is always near, guiding us, and giving us the courage to make choices that honor Him. This promise encourages us to rely on His strength, to seek His help, and to trust that He is greater than any temptation we may face. God's deliverance from temptation doesn't mean that we won't face struggles, but it does mean that every struggle has a way of escape, a path that leads back to His love and His will for our lives. We can face each temptation with confidence, knowing that God's power within us is greater than anything that tries to pull us away from Him. Through His deliverance,

we find freedom from the chains of sin, the strength to resist, and the peace of knowing that God's faithfulness will always carry us through. Each time we overcome a temptation, we grow stronger in faith, closer to God, and more certain of His power at work in our lives. This promise is a beacon of hope, a reminder that no matter what we face, God is with us, faithfully providing a way out and leading us toward victory.

Chapter 26 - Discerning His Will

In Romans 12:2, we find an invitation from God that is both powerful and life-changing: "Be ye transformed by the renewing of your mind, that ye may prove what is that good, and acceptable, and perfect, will of God." This verse reveals the heart of God's desire for each of us—to walk in His will, to understand His purpose for our lives, and to live in a way that reflects His love and truth. The path to Discerning His Will is one that involves a complete transformation of how we think, how we see the world, and how we understand our lives in light of His purpose. Discerning God's will is not something that happens all at once; it's a journey, a daily process of drawing closer to Him, letting go of our own limited ways, and allowing His Spirit to renew our hearts and minds. This kind of transformation doesn't come from simply following the patterns of the world or the advice of others; it comes from surrendering our minds to God, inviting Him to shape our thoughts, and trusting Him to guide us.

To renew our minds means to replace our old ways of thinking with God's truth, to let His Word fill our hearts, and to allow His Spirit to reshape our desires, our goals, and our understanding of life. This transformation is essential for discerning His will because it aligns our minds with His heart, allowing us to see things through His perspective. In a world filled with distractions, noise, and pressures, discerning God's will requires us to quiet our souls and seek His voice above all else. It means choosing to step away from the constant pull of the world and to focus on what God is saying to us personally. God's will is not hidden from us; He desires for us to know it, to seek it diligently, and to walk in it with confidence. But to do this, we must be willing to let Him change us, to renew our thoughts, and to transform our lives from the inside out. God's will for each of us is good, acceptable, and perfect, and He longs for us to experience the fullness of life that comes from following His path.

As we open our hearts to this transformation, we begin to understand that God's will is rooted in His love and His purpose for our lives. It's not about rules or restrictions; it's about a relationship with Him, one that brings us joy, peace, and a sense of purpose. Discerning His will involves trusting that His plans for us are always for our good, even when we can't see the whole picture. It means letting go of our fears, our doubts, and our desires to control everything, and choosing instead to rely on His wisdom and His timing. Each time we allow God to renew our minds, we become more sensitive to His voice, more aware of His presence, and more open to the direction He has for us. His will becomes clearer, not because He changes, but because our hearts and minds become more attuned to His Spirit.

This journey of discerning God's will is also a journey of faith. It requires us to step out, even when we don't have all the answers, and to trust that God is guiding us. We may not always understand why certain doors close or why some paths are harder than others, but we can be confident that God's will is leading us toward His best for us. Discerning His will is not about having a perfect road map; it's about walking in step with Him, trusting that each step brings us closer to His purpose. God's will is always for our good, shaped by His wisdom, and guided by His understanding of who we are and what we need. When we seek His will with a renewed mind, we are able to see beyond our own limited view and to trust in His greater plan.

Living in God's will also brings a peace that goes beyond our circumstances. When we know we are walking in His purpose, we can face challenges with a calm confidence, knowing that He is with us. This peace comes from the assurance that we are exactly where we are meant to be, doing what God has called us to do. It frees us from the need to compare ourselves to others, to worry about the future, or to strive for things that are not part of His plan for us. With a renewed mind, we see the beauty of God's will, recognizing that His ways are higher than our ways and that His thoughts are higher than our thoughts. We learn to trust Him fully, knowing that He is leading us toward a life filled with meaning, purpose, and grace.

Discerning God's will requires patience and a willingness to wait on His timing. There will be moments when we feel uncertain, when the path ahead seems unclear, but these are the times when we can lean into His presence and seek His guidance even more. God's will often unfolds step by step, revealing itself as we continue to trust Him and move forward in faith. This process strengthens our relationship with Him, teaching us to rely on His faithfulness and to listen for His gentle whispers. In these moments, we learn that discerning His will is not about having all the answers, but about walking in a relationship with Him, allowing Him to lead us one step at a time.

God's will is not just about what we do; it's about who we are becoming. As we allow Him to renew our minds, He shapes our character, helping us to grow in love, patience, kindness, and humility. Discerning His will transforms us, making us more like Christ and enabling us to live lives that reflect His love and light to those around us. It's a transformation that impacts not only our choices but also our relationships, our attitudes, and our purpose. Each day, as we seek His will, we are reminded that our lives are part of a bigger story, one that is woven together by His love and grace. We find fulfillment not in following our own plans, but in surrendering to His perfect plan, knowing that His will is always good, acceptable, and perfect.

Discerning God's will is a journey of surrender, a daily decision to let go of our own desires and to embrace His purpose for our lives. It's a journey that brings us closer to His heart, helping us to understand His love and to experience the peace that comes from living in His presence. As we allow Him to renew our minds, we are filled with a sense of clarity and purpose, knowing that we are walking in step with the One who created us. This journey is not always easy, but it is always worth it, for it leads us to a life that is rich in meaning, filled with joy, and anchored in God's love.

The more we seek God's will, the more we come to understand that His plans for us are greater than anything we could imagine. His will brings us hope, gives us strength, and fills us with a sense of purpose that goes beyond ourselves. We begin to see our lives through His eyes, recognizing that we are part of His greater plan. This understanding gives us the courage to step out in faith, to take risks, and to trust that God is guiding us, even when the path is uncertain. His will is not just about our personal happiness; it's about His glory, His kingdom, and His purpose for the world. As we align our hearts with His, we find that our desires begin to reflect His desires, our dreams begin to align with His purpose, and our lives become a reflection of His love.

Discerning God's will also brings us closer to His truth, helping us to stand firm in our faith and to live with integrity. When we know that we are walking in His purpose, we are less likely to be swayed by the opinions of others or by the pressures of the world. We find strength in His Word, guidance in His Spirit, and peace in His presence. God's will becomes a source of stability in our lives, a foundation that holds us steady in times of uncertainty and change. This foundation gives us confidence, helping us to live boldly, to love deeply, and to serve faithfully, knowing that we are exactly where God wants us to be.

The journey of discerning God's will is one of transformation, growth, and trust. It's a journey that leads us to a life that is filled with purpose, peace, and joy. Each day, as we seek His guidance, we are reminded that God's will is not a destination but a path, a way of living that brings us closer to Him and fills our lives with meaning. We don't have to have all the answers, for we know the One who does. His will is our guide, His Word is our light, and His Spirit is our strength, leading us toward a life that honors Him and reflects His love.

Chapter 27 - Divine Patience

In 2 Peter 3:9, we are given one of the most comforting insights into the heart of God: "The Lord is not slack concerning his promise... but is longsuffering to us-ward." These words reveal the depth and beauty of Divine Patience—God's incredible and steadfast willingness to wait for us, to extend grace upon grace, and to hold back judgment, even when we falter, because He loves us so deeply. God's patience is not like ours; it is perfect, enduring, and unfailing, a patience filled with mercy, kindness, and boundless love. When we talk about Divine Patience, we are speaking of a God who, despite all our weaknesses, our failures, and our struggles, does not give up on us. Imagine the Creator of the universe, the One who crafted everything from the stars in the heavens to the smallest details of our lives, waiting patiently for each one of us. He knows every aspect of our lives, every detail, every misstep, yet He waits. His patience is so profound that it goes beyond our understanding. Where we might quickly judge, lose hope, or grow frustrated with others—or even ourselves—God's patience remains steady and unwavering. He is committed to waiting because He sees who we are meant to be, and He believes in the potential within each of us.

God's patience is not a sign of delay or hesitation; it is a demonstration of His desire for us to come to Him freely, to seek His love, and to find redemption in His embrace. In His patience, we find a love so pure and so enduring that it stays with us even through our darkest moments, offering hope, forgiveness, and the chance to start again. Divine Patience is God's way of showing us that He values our growth, our understanding, and our willingness to come to Him, no matter where we are on our journey. He does not impose Himself but waits, gently calling us, guiding us, and giving us countless opportunities to respond to His love. His patience allows us the time to recognize His goodness, to experience His mercy, and to be transformed by

His presence. It is a patience that understands our struggles, our fears, and our questions, and that gives us the space to learn, to heal, and to grow.

God's patience is not a passive thing; it is active, always present, and filled with His enduring love. Every moment of patience God extends to us is an invitation—a call to come closer, to trust in Him, and to embrace the life He offers. He does not rush us but walks with us through every valley, every trial, and every moment of doubt. His patience reminds us that He is not distant or uninvolved but is deeply invested in our lives, constantly working behind the scenes to bring us closer to Him. He knows every part of us and understands our unique journey, our personal challenges, and our need for His guidance. Divine Patience is God's assurance that He will never give up on us, no matter how many times we may stumble or fall. When we feel that we've drifted too far or that we're beyond redemption, God's patience is there, showing us that His love has no limits, that His mercy is endless, and that His heart is always open to us.

In His patience, we are reminded of the depth of His grace. Where others might judge, criticize, or abandon, God chooses to wait, to forgive, and to restore. His patience is a source of hope, a reminder that no matter how many times we fall, we are never too far from His reach. God's patience gives us the courage to try again, to believe that we are worth the effort, and to understand that His love for us is greater than any mistake we could ever make. Each day, His patience offers us a new beginning, a fresh start, and the chance to live more fully in His love. It is an open door, inviting us to walk with Him, to learn from Him, and to experience the peace that comes from knowing we are held in His hands. Divine Patience is God's way of saying that He values our journey, that He understands our need for time, and that He is committed to us, no matter what.

God's patience is also a reflection of His faithfulness to His promises. He is not slow in keeping His word; instead, He waits so that we can grow, so that we can understand, and so that we can freely choose to follow Him. His patience shows that He respects our freedom, allowing us to come to Him in our own time, not forcing us but drawing us with love. Divine Patience is a profound expression of God's respect for us, His children, showing us that He values our journey and wants us to come to Him willingly. It is a patience that trusts in His perfect timing, knowing that every moment we spend growing in faith, every lesson we learn, and every step we take toward Him brings us closer to His heart. God's patience is filled with compassion, understanding our weaknesses and knowing that growth takes time.

Each moment of patience God extends to us is filled with His grace and kindness, a reminder that His love is unconditional and that He sees beyond our failures. He knows who we can become through His guidance and love. His patience is a gift, giving us the time to understand His ways, to experience His mercy, and to grow in faith. God's patience is also a lesson for us, teaching us to be patient with others and with ourselves. It reminds us that just as God waits for us, we, too, can learn to wait for His timing, trusting that His plans are good and that His purposes will come to pass in His perfect way. Divine Patience encourages us to walk in faith, knowing that God's timing is always right, even when we don't understand it.

God's patience also teaches us about forgiveness. In His patience, we see a God who does not hold our mistakes against us, who does not count our sins, but who is always ready to forgive, to restore, and to renew. His patience reminds us that we are loved not because of what we do, but because of who we are—His beloved children. This patience is a reflection of His endless mercy, a mercy that wipes away our past and gives us a future filled with hope. It is a patience that encourages us to come to Him boldly, knowing that He will never turn us away. Divine Patience is a source of strength, helping us to trust in His love, to rely on His grace, and to believe that He is always with us, no matter what.

In a world that often rushes, judges, and expects instant results, God's patience is a refreshing reminder that true love waits, that true grace forgives, and that true mercy is always willing to give another chance. God's patience is not a delay; it is an opportunity, a chance for us to grow, to learn, and to experience His love more deeply. His patience is a constant invitation, calling us to draw near, to seek His face, and to live in the peace that comes from knowing we are cherished. Divine Patience is God's way of saying that we are worth the wait, that He believes in us, and that He is committed to our journey.

Every moment of patience God shows us is filled with His wisdom, His love, and His hope for our future. His patience reminds us that we are never alone, that we are always held in His hands, and that He will never give up on us. It gives us the courage to keep moving forward, to believe in His promises, and to trust that His plans for us are good. Divine Patience is a reminder that we are loved by a God who sees our potential, who knows our worth, and who is willing to wait as long as it takes for us to come to Him. This patience is a source of peace, a promise of His presence, and a testament to His unfailing love.

In His patience, we find a love that is stronger than any fear, a grace that covers every failure, and a hope that fills us with joy. Divine Patience is God's way of showing us that we are cherished, that we are important to Him, and that He is always with us, guiding us, loving us, and leading us toward His perfect plan. His patience is a promise that He will never leave us, that He will never forsake us, and that He will always be there, waiting with open arms, ready to welcome us home.

Chapter 28 - Desire for Righteousness

In Matthew 5:6, Jesus offers a promise that stirs the heart and calls us to a higher purpose: "Blessed are they which do hunger and thirst after righteousness: for they shall be filled." These words are about the Desire for Righteousness—a longing to live in a way that pleases God, to walk in His ways, and to be filled with His goodness. To hunger and thirst for righteousness means more than just wanting to be good or moral; it's a deep, powerful craving to live a life that reflects God's heart, His love, and His truth. Just as our bodies need food and water to survive, our souls need the nourishment that only righteousness can bring. When we truly desire righteousness, we are seeking God Himself, longing to be close to Him, to understand His ways, and to be shaped by His presence. This hunger is not satisfied by the temporary things of this world but only by the eternal love and holiness of God. It's a desire that drives us to pray, to seek, to grow, and to let go of anything that pulls us away from His path. And Jesus promises that those who hunger and thirst after righteousness will be filled—they will find what they are searching for, and they will be satisfied.

To desire righteousness is to yearn for a life that is free from the chains of sin, a life that shines with the light of God's truth, and a heart that is pure and undivided. It's the kind of desire that transforms us from the inside out, changing not only our actions but our thoughts, our motives, and our entire way of being. When we hunger for righteousness, we are opening our hearts to God's guidance, inviting Him to lead us, to correct us, and to teach us how to live in a way that brings glory to His name. This desire for righteousness doesn't mean we are perfect; it means we are willing to grow, willing to learn, and willing to be transformed by God's love and grace. It's a lifelong journey, one that brings us closer to Him each day, filling us with His peace, His strength, and His joy.

God honors this hunger for righteousness because it is a reflection of His own heart. He created us to live in fellowship with Him, to walk in His ways, and to be a light in the world. When we desire righteousness, we are aligning ourselves with His purpose, embracing His standards, and choosing to live according to His will. And Jesus promises that this desire will not go unanswered. He assures us that those who seek will find, that those who knock will have the door opened, and that those who hunger and thirst for righteousness will be filled. This filling is not a one-time experience but a continuous gift, a daily provision of His presence, His wisdom, and His love. Each time we come to Him with open hearts, seeking to live rightly, He meets us, strengthens us, and fills us with His Spirit.

This desire for righteousness fuels our relationship with God, drawing us closer to Him and helping us to become more like Christ. It leads us to forgive, to love, to serve, and to live selflessly, reflecting the character of Jesus in all we do. This desire changes how we see the world, how we treat others, and how we respond to challenges. It fills us with a deep sense of purpose, knowing that we are living not for ourselves but for God's glory. The more we hunger for righteousness, the more we find that God Himself is our fulfillment, our joy, and our strength. This hunger is a gift, a sign that God is working in our hearts, drawing us into a closer walk with Him, and preparing us for a life of blessing and impact.

Desiring righteousness is also about letting go of the things that hinder us from God's best. It's a willingness to surrender our selfish desires, our pride, and our need for control, and to trust that God's ways are better than our own. When we hunger for righteousness, we are saying to God, "Change me, mold me, and fill me with Your presence." This desire leads us to repentance, to humility, and to a deeper understanding of His grace. It reminds us that we cannot achieve righteousness on our own but need His help, His guidance, and His Spirit. And in His mercy, God answers this hunger with His unfailing love, drawing near to us and filling us with His peace. The satisfaction we find in His righteousness is unlike anything the world can offer; it is lasting, fulfilling, and life-changing.

To hunger and thirst for righteousness is to live with an unquenchable desire for God, to seek His face, to know His heart, and to walk in His truth. This hunger drives us to spend time in His Word, to pray, and to seek His presence in every part of our lives. It is a desire that brings us hope, that fills us with courage, and that helps us to stand firm, even in a world that may not understand our faith. Each day, as we seek His righteousness, we are filled with a deeper sense of His love, a clearer understanding of His purpose, and a greater strength to live out our faith. Jesus promises that those who hunger for righteousness will be filled, not just temporarily, but with a lasting fulfillment that comes from knowing we are living in the center of God's will.

This desire for righteousness is the foundation of a life that honors God, a life that is set apart, and a life that makes a difference in the world. It is the fuel for our faith, the reason for our hope, and the source of our joy. When we desire righteousness, we are choosing to live in the light, to walk in truth, and to be an example of God's love to those around us. This hunger brings us closer to God, fills us with His Spirit, and equips us to face whatever life brings with faith and confidence. It is a journey that brings us joy, fulfillment, and peace, knowing that we are living for something greater than ourselves.

The promise that we will be filled is a testament to God's faithfulness. He sees our desire, He knows our hearts, and He honors our pursuit of righteousness by filling us with His presence, His love, and His peace. This filling is a gift, a daily blessing that sustains us, strengthens us, and guides us. Each day, as we seek Him, He fills us anew, providing everything we need to live a life that glorifies Him. This promise is a source of hope, a reminder that our efforts are not in vain, and that God's presence is always with us, helping us, guiding us, and loving us every step of the way.

Desiring righteousness is a lifelong journey, one that brings us closer to God and helps us to grow in faith, in love, and in grace. It is a journey that shapes us, molds us, and fills us with a purpose that goes beyond ourselves. As we continue to seek Him, to hunger for His truth, and to live in His love, we find that our lives are filled with His goodness, His peace, and His joy. This desire for righteousness is not about being perfect; it's about being willing to grow, to learn, and to let God's love transform us from the inside out.

Chapter 29 - Delivered from Darkness

In Colossians 1:13, we find a powerful message of hope and freedom: "Who hath delivered us from the power of darkness, and hath translated us into the kingdom of his dear Son." This verse is about being Delivered from Darkness, a miraculous transformation that only God can perform. When we talk about darkness, we're talking about everything that holds us back, everything that keeps us in fear, in sin, in doubt, and in hopelessness. Darkness is that place where we feel lost, trapped, and unable to see the way forward. But God, in His incredible love, reaches into that darkness, into the very depths of our struggles, and pulls us out, delivering us from everything that tries to hold us down. Through Jesus, we are no longer prisoners of the darkness; we are free. God's deliverance means we don't have to stay in our past, bound by mistakes or trapped in cycles of guilt and shame. He has taken us out of the grasp of darkness and has placed us in the light of His kingdom, the kingdom of His dear Son, where love, hope, and grace abound. This isn't just a temporary escape; it's a complete rescue, a transformation from death to life, from hopelessness to hope, from fear to faith. To be delivered from darkness means that God has broken every chain, shattered every barrier, and freed us from the power that darkness once held over us. He has done what we could never do for ourselves, giving us a new life, a new purpose, and a new identity as His children. We are no longer defined by our failures, by our fears, or by the things that once kept us bound. We are now part of His kingdom, a kingdom filled with love, joy, and peace, where we can live in the light of His truth and in the fullness of His grace. God didn't just take us out of darkness; He brought us into something far greater—the kingdom of His Son, where we are loved, accepted, and valued. In this kingdom, we find purpose, we find belonging, and we find a life that is so much greater than anything the darkness could ever offer. Being delivered from darkness is a reminder that God's power is greater than any force of evil, that His love is stronger than any fear, and that His light will always outshine the darkness. Each day, as we live in the light of His kingdom, we are filled with gratitude, knowing that we have been saved, redeemed, and set free. This deliverance gives us hope in every situation, courage to face any challenge, and a joy that cannot be taken away. God's deliverance from darkness is not just a moment; it's an eternal promise, a constant assurance that we belong to Him, and that nothing can ever pull us back into the darkness we once knew. We are children of the light, called to live boldly, to walk in faith, and to shine His love into a world that so desperately needs it. Being delivered from darkness means that we can live each day with the assurance that God is with us, that He is for us, and that His light will guide us every step of the way.

Chapter 30 - Divine Assurance

In Romans 8:28, we find one of the most powerful and comforting promises in the entire Bible: "And we know that all things work together for good to them that love God." These words offer us Divine Assurance—a deep, unshakable confidence that God is actively working in every part of our lives. No matter what we face, God is present, weaving every joy and every challenge into a tapestry of grace and purpose. Divine Assurance is knowing that nothing in our lives is wasted, that every experience, every struggle, and every victory is being used for a greater good. When we feel lost, uncertain, or overwhelmed, this promise assures us that God's hand is guiding us, holding us, and carefully directing every detail for our benefit. Divine Assurance does not mean life will be free from hardship; instead, it promises that God's purpose will prevail through it all. It tells us that every tear, every prayer, and every heartbreak matters to Him and is part of a grand design that leads to our ultimate good.

Imagine a life where every setback, every failure, and every sorrow is being transformed by God into something beautiful and meaningful. That is what Divine Assurance is about—knowing that God takes everything, even the things we don't understand or can't see a way through, and turns it into a blessing in His time. We may face disappointments and challenges, but Divine Assurance means that God's purpose for us is never in jeopardy. He sees the bigger picture, the complete tapestry of our lives, when we can only see the individual threads. This assurance gives us peace in the midst of uncertainty because we know we are in the hands of a loving Father who does not waste a single moment of our journey.

Divine Assurance tells us that God's timing is perfect, that He knows exactly what we need and when we need it. When things don't go as we planned or when life feels chaotic, we can trust that He is orchestrating every event, every encounter, and every step for a purpose beyond what we can imagine.

We might face situations that seem insurmountable or moments that make us question why, but this assurance reminds us that God is working behind the scenes. Even when we cannot see it, His hand is moving, arranging everything according to His perfect plan. Divine Assurance is like an anchor in the storm, keeping us steady even when the waves are high and the winds are fierce. It is the calm in our hearts, the quiet certainty that we are not walking through life alone but with a God who is both mighty and loving.

This assurance doesn't come from our circumstances; it comes from knowing God's character. He is faithful, and He is good, and His promises are always true. Divine Assurance tells us that He is not just aware of our struggles; He is deeply involved, carefully guiding us through each one. Every time we face a challenge, God uses it to strengthen our faith, to draw us closer to Him, and to prepare us for what lies ahead. This promise of Divine Assurance gives us hope that nothing we go through is in vain. God sees our pain, understands our fears, and cares about our dreams. He works in all things, both big and small, to accomplish His purpose for our lives. With Divine Assurance, we can face each day with courage, knowing that no matter what happens, God is with us, and He is working all things together for good.

In the midst of trials, Divine Assurance reminds us that we are never alone. God's presence is constant, His love is unending, and His purpose for our lives cannot be shaken. Even in moments of doubt or fear, we can cling to the truth that God's plan is unbreakable. He holds us in His hands, guiding us with wisdom and compassion. Divine Assurance tells us that God's promises are not dependent on our strength or ability; they are anchored in His power and faithfulness. He has committed to us, and His love is steadfast, carrying us through every storm and lifting us above every challenge. In times of joy, we see His blessings clearly, and in times of sorrow, we feel His comforting presence.

Divine Assurance gives us a foundation of peace and security that nothing in this world can take away. It tells us that we don't have to have all the answers or know every step of the journey. We only need to trust the One who does. God's love for us is so deep that He uses every moment of our lives to shape us, to teach us, and to bring us closer to Him. This assurance gives us the freedom to let go of worry and to rest in His promises. We may face setbacks, but Divine Assurance tells us that God is still in control, still faithful, and still working on our behalf.

With Divine Assurance, we know that God's purpose is far greater than our present struggles. This promise encourages us to live with hope, to persevere in faith, and to hold onto the truth that God is always with us. When we don't understand why things happen, Divine Assurance reminds us that God sees the full picture and that He is crafting something beautiful out of every experience. Each difficulty, each challenge, and each unexpected turn is being used by God to refine us, to build our character, and to deepen our faith. This promise gives us strength, resilience, and a joy that endures through every season.

Divine Assurance is knowing that, as we walk with God, every step, every decision, and every prayer is part of a greater story that He is writing. We are not alone, not forgotten, and not forsaken. God is with us, guiding us, loving us, and working in ways that we may not see or understand right now. But one day, we will look back and see how His hand was in every detail, how His love covered every moment, and how His purpose was fulfilled in ways more wonderful than we could have imagined. Divine Assurance is the reminder that our lives are held securely in the hands of a God who is both sovereign and compassionate, a God who promises to work all things together for our good.

This assurance fills us with a peace that surpasses understanding, a peace that remains even when circumstances are challenging. It encourages us to keep moving forward, to keep trusting, and to keep believing that God's plan is good. Divine Assurance is the hope that carries us through every trial, the strength that sustains us in every weakness, and the joy that lifts us in every sorrow. It is the foundation upon which we build our lives, the rock upon which we stand, and the light that guides us in the darkness. In this promise, we find a love that never fails, a grace that is always sufficient, and a faithfulness that endures forever.

As we hold onto this Divine Assurance, we are reminded that we are never alone in our journey. God is with us, walking beside us, guiding us, and working in every detail. His promises are true, His love is constant, and His purpose for our lives is unshakeable. Divine Assurance gives us the confidence to live boldly, to love deeply, and to trust fully in the One who has promised to work all things together for good. It is a promise that fills us with hope, strengthens our faith, and reminds us that we are deeply loved by a God who will never leave us or forsake us.

Chapter 31 - Depth of His Compassion

In Psalm 103:13, we are given a glimpse into the unfathomable heart of God: "Like as a father pitieth his children, so the LORD pitieth them that fear him." This verse reveals the Depth of His Compassion—a boundless, unwavering compassion that reaches out to us in ways we can barely understand, yet which fills us with a profound sense of comfort, hope, and love. Imagine a parent's love for their child, the tenderness, the fierce protectiveness, and the endless patience they offer. But God's compassion toward us surpasses even this. His love for us is greater than any earthly love, stronger than any human understanding, and so gentle that it meets us exactly where we are, no matter how low or broken we may feel. His compassion is like the warmth of a parent holding their child close, feeling every pain, every joy, every hope, and every sorrow along with them. It is a compassion that doesn't turn away when we fail, when we make mistakes, or when we are hurting; instead, it draws even closer, embracing us with love, healing, and forgiveness. The depth of His compassion is so complete that He knows our hearts better than we know ourselves, understanding every part of us, even the parts we keep hidden. He understands our struggles, our weaknesses, and our fears, yet He never grows weary of us, never turns away, and never leaves us alone.

God's compassion means that He is always ready to comfort, guide, and uplift us. Like a father who watches over his children, God is attentive to every detail of our lives. His compassion doesn't overlook us, doesn't ignore our cries, but meets us in every place of need, providing a love that is constant and true. When we are filled with joy, He rejoices with us; when we face sorrow, He shares in our grief; and when we are in pain, His heart aches with ours. His compassion is so deep that it reaches into the darkest parts of our lives, bringing light, healing, and hope. We are never alone in our struggles, never left to face life on our own, because His compassion surrounds us, holds us, and lifts us up. The depth of His compassion is like a warm embrace that assures us we are safe, loved, and understood. God's compassion is not passive or distant; it is an active, present love that moves Him to act on our behalf, to provide for us, to protect us, and to offer us grace upon grace.

In our moments of weakness, God's compassion is our strength, a strength that doesn't scold us for our failures but gently guides us forward. When we fall, His compassion lifts us up, dusts us off, and encourages us to keep going. He doesn't focus on our mistakes but on our potential, seeing us as beloved children whom He is eager to help, nurture, and grow. This depth of compassion is so incredible that it even forgives us when we stumble, showing mercy that goes beyond our understanding. His compassion doesn't hold our past against us but offers us a fresh start, a new beginning, and a path forward that is filled with His love and grace. He is like a father who celebrates every step we take, every effort we make, always ready to encourage and support us as we walk with Him.

God's compassion is a shelter, a place of refuge where we can find rest for our weary souls. In a world that can be harsh, unforgiving, and full of pressure, God's compassion provides a sanctuary, a safe place where we are accepted just as we are. We don't have to pretend or hide our weaknesses; we can come to Him openly, knowing that His compassion welcomes us, understands us, and loves us unconditionally. His compassion is patient with us, never growing frustrated when we struggle, but gently guiding us with kindness and love. When we feel lost, God's compassion becomes our guide, lighting the way and reminding us that we are never too far gone, never too broken, and never beyond His reach. This depth of compassion is a reminder that God sees us not just for who we are now but for who we can become through His love and grace.

The compassion of God is so great that it moved Him to send His Son to save us, to bridge the gap that sin had created and to bring us back to Him. Jesus' life, death, and resurrection are the ultimate expressions of God's compassion, a compassion that would sacrifice everything to ensure that we could be with Him forever. This act of love shows us just how far God's compassion will go, reaching into the very depths of our brokenness to offer us redemption, hope, and new life. His compassion doesn't just cover our past; it transforms our future, giving us a purpose, a calling, and a place in His family.

Through His compassion, we are not just forgiven but adopted, chosen, and cherished. We become His children, loved with an everlasting love, guided by His gentle hand, and protected by His strength.

Each day, as we experience His compassion, we are reminded of how deeply He cares for us. His compassion is not conditional, not based on what we do or how well we perform; it is a gift, freely given, and it is ours to embrace. The depth of His compassion is a constant assurance that we are never alone, that we are always loved, and that we are forever held in His hands. Even when the world seems uncertain, even when we feel weak, His compassion is a steady presence, a reminder that we are His and that He will never let us go. This compassion gives us courage to face life's challenges, knowing that we are not facing them on our own. God is with us, carrying us when we are weary, comforting us when we are hurting, and celebrating with us in every moment of joy.

In His compassion, we find a love that is beyond measure, a love that cannot be earned or lost, a love that is as steady as the rising sun and as constant as the stars. The depth of His compassion fills us with hope, reminding us that no matter what we go through, we are never without His presence. God's compassion is our anchor, a foundation of love that holds us steady even in life's storms. When we are afraid, His compassion is our peace; when we are uncertain, His compassion is our confidence; and when we are broken, His compassion is our healing. He is a Father who watches over us, who knows every detail of our lives, and who cares for us with a love that has no end.

God's compassion is also an invitation, a call to come closer, to know Him more deeply, and to trust in His love. It invites us to lay down our burdens, to surrender our fears, and to rest in the assurance that we are loved, seen, and cherished by our Creator. His compassion teaches us to love others as He loves us, to show kindness, patience, and forgiveness, reflecting His heart in all we do. The depth of His compassion transforms us, helping us to see the world through His eyes and to live with a heart that beats in tune with His. As we experience His compassion, we are changed, becoming more like Him, more loving, more patient, and more willing to serve those around us.

This compassion is a reminder that God's love is always near, always available, and always ready to meet us wherever we are. In every moment, in every season, His compassion is there, guiding us, comforting us, and filling us with hope. The depth of His compassion is a gift beyond measure, a love that will never fail, and a promise that we are His forever. It gives us strength in weakness, joy in sorrow, and peace in the midst of life's challenges. No matter where we go, no matter what we face, we can be confident that the depth of God's compassion will always be with us, a constant reminder that we are His beloved children, cherished and held in His everlasting arms.

Conclusion

As we come to the end of "Unshakeable Faith: 31 Days of Peace in God's Word," let this journey be just the beginning of a life anchored in God's promises. Over these days, we've seen how God's Word is a steady, unfailing source of peace, no matter the storms we face. This isn't just a lesson for a month; it's a call to live each day rooted in the truth of who God is and what He promises. When fears rise and worries creep in, remember that God's peace isn't something we earn; it's a gift He freely gives to those who trust Him. Being a Christian doesn't mean that life will be easy, but it does mean we don't face it alone. As you move forward, carry the strength, comfort, and confidence that comes from knowing God walks with you. Let the peace we've found in His Word be a shield around your heart, guarding you when challenges arise and strengthening you when the path seems uncertain. Every day, renew your trust in Him, taking the steps of faith He calls you to, even when the way is unclear. Let your faith grow unshakeable as you remember that God's love for you is greater than any fear, and His power is more than enough to meet every need. Continue to make space for God's Word, letting it refresh your heart and remind you of His promises. Let prayer be your lifeline, drawing you closer to the One who understands your every need and stands ready to help. Keep choosing peace, keep choosing trust, and keep choosing to stand on His promises. Know that even when the world shifts and troubles come, you can rest in the assurance that God is with you, His peace will guide you, and His strength will hold you. Carry this unshakeable faith with you, knowing that your life is in the hands of a faithful God who will never fail you. Let His peace be your constant, your hope, and your strength in all things.

Don't miss out!

Visit the website below and you can sign up to receive emails whenever Joshua Rhoades publishes a new book. There's no charge and no obligation.

https://books2read.com/r/B-A-AJLBB-HHSDF

BOOKS 2 READ

Connecting independent readers to independent writers.

Did you love *Unshakeable Faith- 31 Days of Peace in God's Word*? Then you should read *Answer The Call - 31 Days of Biblical Action*[1] by Joshua Rhoades!

[2]

"Answer the Call – 31 Days of Biblical Action" is a transformative devotional that challenges you to not only read the Word of God but to live it every day. This powerful 31-day guide is uniquely centered around individual action verbs drawn from Scripture, calling you to apply specific actions in your daily life. Each day highlights a verb—such as love, serve, forgive, trust, or pray—and encourages you to engage deeply with its biblical meaning while putting it into practice.

This is not just a devotional for reflection; it's a call to action, a stirring reminder that faith is most alive when it moves. By focusing on one verb each day, "Answer the Call" helps you to integrate the teachings of the Bible into your daily routine, bringing the message of Scripture to life in practical and meaningful ways.

---

1. https://books2read.com/u/4X5kG9

2. https://books2read.com/u/4X5kG9

The book invites you to engage your heart and hands as you follow Christ's example. Each action verb acts as a catalyst for spiritual growth, reminding you that faith isn't static but dynamic and responsive. Whether it's through acts of kindness, moments of prayer, or stepping out in faith, these daily challenges will inspire you to live out your beliefs with boldness and purpose.

By the end of the 31 days, you will feel encouraged, empowered, and renewed. "Answer the Call" will leave you transformed, ready to live your faith in real, actionable ways, embodying the teachings of Scripture in every area of your life.